THEOLOGICAL HANDBOOK ON EMOTIONS

DR. GERRY WHITE

Theological Handbook of Emotion

Printed by CreateSpace

Estore link: www.createspace.com/3487048

Library of congress Catalog-in-Publishing Data

White, Gerry, D.

1. PSY013000 – Psychology/Emotions – Textbook. / White, Gerry, D.

   Includes Biographical references and index.

   ISBN: 0-9-797776-1-5

   ISBN-13: 978-0-9797776-1-5

   Library of Congress Control Number: 2010916717

Unless otherwise noted, all Quick Scripture reference are from the New King James Version.

Unless otherwise noted, all Scripture quotations are from the Holy Bible, King James Version.

Unless otherwise noted, all Hebrew and Greek words and their meanings have come from the Strong's Exhaustive Concordance of the Bible

Unless otherwise noted, all definitions of terms have come from Merriam-Webster's Collegiate Dictionary, (11th Ed.).

Printed in the United States of America 2010.

DEDICATION

This book is dedicated to my wife, Melanie and daughter, Chloe'. I am humbled to have two "best friends". They are my life. No journey of life is quite complete without a friend to travel with you. God has richly blessed me with two. I am grateful for their love and kindness.

CONTENTS

"All my springs are in you" Psalm 87:7

Introduction – Why am I writing this book on emotion?

In my research of journal articles and books published on emotion, I have found theories which postulate the etiology of emotion in brain mapping. In two books, the *Handbook of Emotions*, and the *Handbook of Emotion Regulation*, authors have theorized emotional etiology has emerged from the human brain. Most recently, Joseph LeDoux, the author of the *Emotional Brain*, theorizes the pre-synaptic and post-synaptic activity is the magic formula to understand the synaptic self.

In this book I have tried to separate brain origination theory from biblical presuppositions showing the significance of the spirit in man which is fully embodied in human flesh. I have used the Greek and Hebrew language to specifically validate emotion etiology. This research uses both the Old Testament and New Testament to fully explain how human beings have emotion.

In the late 1800's very little theological writing was published to establish an authoritative view of emotion. Some philosophers like Plato, Aristotle, and Socrates continued debating the spirit of man as they understood the complexity of the human being. Moreover, when psychologists began publishing their theories in the 1930's, the theological presses became silenced to the mounting psychological research. The best accounting of integration of psychology and theology that I have read is in a book entitled "*The Integration of Psychology and Theology*" by John Carter and Bruce Narramore. Without repeating this book to explain how and why integration is taking place, I have added just a few more comments by scholars in the field.

Even in the medical field, there is an enlarging disconnect to the spirit of man. Palmer (2003) suggested there is a need for spirituality in a secular society especially in medical education. A new commitment to build a network of change will help medicine reclaim its integrity. He suggested clinical evidence is increasingly clear that physicians who cannot connect with the "heart and soul" of the patient are less likely to be healers than those who can; a physician who has no access to his or her own inner life cannot possibly get access to the patient's inner life; physicians who lose touch with their own identity and integrity cannot speak the truth to power amid institutional dynamics that threaten to undermine their Hippocratic oath; and thoughtful physician leaders fear that their profession is "losing its soul".

Palmer (et. al) added society's expectation was growing and found similar discussions in public education. He continued by saying, "framing inner life issues in ways hospitable to diversity is clearly critical if we want to help people in the public world rejoin 'soul and role.' A pedagogy of the soul challenges conventional academic approaches".

Helminiak (1996) found the American Psychological Association added spirituality to the index terms listed in the PsycLIT computerized database. This approach allows for a rigorous and normative treatment of spiritual issues apart from all theological implications. This allowed a fully humanist account of spirit plus a position on interdisciplinary method combine and generates a scientific approach to spirituality. The human spirit was distinctly labeled human consciousness, including experience, understanding, judgment, and decision. The human psyche included imagery, memory, and emotion. Instead of designating a trichotomy of being, psychology adopted a dichotomy view which distinguished psyche and spirit within mind.

Towns (2001) described the differences in trichotomy and dichotomy of the human being. Basically, man is composed of three separate substances: body, soul, and spirit (trichotomy), verses a body and soul (dichotomy) model. In this book I have explained the spirit in depth. Body includes the human flesh or material substance. Soul encompasses the three dimensional being. Spirit is the life of the person.

In order to understand the dynamic of spirit, the reader is encouraged to read the whole text assimilating all parts in order to understand the whole of spirit. Months of research have been completed included reading texts, journals, and online library searches to aid in the treatment of this subject.

APPRECIATING THEOLOGY AND PSYCHOLOGY AS AN INTEGRATED WHOLE

In support of this integrative approach, I have illustrated biblical data in Hebrew and Greek to explain aspects of the spirit. Using only the English translation to explain the spirit does not go deep enough to get the root meaning of words and phrases. Some words are defined very well. This will help students reading this book to gain a better understanding. In other words, a more primitive word is given which more specifically defines meaning. In each case where primitive words are listed, they are given after the primary word is used.

The richest meanings of words are then used to explain the spirit. Spirit defined by psychology includes the mind of a human being. Students should not expect usual and customary understandings of spirit as hypothesized in psychology to be the same in this text. A new appreciation of spirit as a separate entity is fully expressed and explained.

The integration of topics, research, and findings across chapters, will sharpen the students understanding of the whole. A solid scriptural foundation is established and used to fully describe an etiological approach before psychological theory is applied. I have paid close attention to current books and journal articles which subject students to research without any theological input. Therefore, students will focus on the theological evidence first in gaining a biblical understanding of the spirit.

When psychology research is included, students will gain a new perspective on how integrated scriptural data is understood without theorizing a modality of etiology. There will be some biblical evidence that enhances (i.e. explains process) or opposes psychological theory of emotion. Students will gain an appreciation for the pathways of emotion.

APPRECIATING THEOLOGY AND PSYCHOLOGY'S UNDERSTANDING OF THE SPIRIT

By the beginning of the twenty-first century, more research has been completed on emotion than most of the twentieth century. Journal writers on emotion research have established norms in psychological theory from current research. Very little research has contrasted the current findings to scriptural data. Students will gain a thorough appreciation for scriptural research into the spirit. Basic presuppositions will be tested and redefined as new understandings are integrated into past theory.

In each chapter I have taken extreme caution to not hypothesize or academically attack views which may contrast opposing views. Where scripture and psychology are in extreme difference, both views are expressed. Moreover, the weakness within observed hypothetical assumption and postulation are differentiated. Such as, psychology is presently building a research model of brain origination to explain where emotions begin. Where scripture data delineates difference, the student may have issue with comparing and contrasting origination.

APPRECIATING HOW SCRIPTURE EXPLAINS THE PROCESS OF HUMAN EMOTION

Students who have read the scriptures in the past may find themselves surprised when they read this textbook on emotion. The depth of exegetical study identifies the etiology and process of human emotion. I assume students already accept the authority and validity of the scriptures. Moreover, I do not attempt to establish a theology of revelation, inspiration, inerrancy, or illumination. If a student is not well studied in the scriptures this textbook includes verses of scripture to be looked up and studied for further insight.

You will notice in each chapter there is a multiplicity of scriptures used to explain and validate the process of human emotion. Most of the verses used are taken from the New King James Version. However, in all cases the English words were looked up in the Strong's Concordance. Whether words were taken from an Old Testament or New Testament scripture, the Hebrew and Greek word definitions were used to gain the richest insight in the meaning of a word or passage of scripture.

APPRECIATING THE HUMAN SPIRIT

To help students appreciate the human spirit from theology and psychology, this textbook has integrated terms and definitions from both areas of study. To appreciate the wealth of scientific research in psychology, counseling terms have been added. A concentration of psychology and counseling terms are used interchangeably. Moreover, students in either fields of study will appreciate the emergence of ideology in descriptive explanations throughout many chapters.

The human spirit is in every human being. Instead of mounting evidence from both fields of study, which would have built an incredible schism, I have tried to show how each descriptors are specific in nature. The scriptures are very specific in describing the human spirit. In psychology several terms are used to describe the human spirit. Students of psychology may have some issue with the convergence of difference from specific areas of scientific research in psychology.

I would highly recommend that each student consider the human spirit as separate from the human whole. When the human whole is studied as one, a student may have difficulty understanding the human spirit as separate. Therefore, taking notes and answering the questions at the end of every chapter may prove helpful. Of all the material in Theology and Psychology, students struggle the most with the area of study they know the least.

Chapter One – Does God speak today?

THROUGHOUT THIS TEXT I SUBMIT instances whereby I have sought very specific answers to questions given to God. Some of my readers have asked if this were "mystical" or "extra biblical revelation"? If it were mystical in nature then it would be impossible to be clear or concise. Asking God questions and receiving answers from Him (Jer. 33:3) is not extra biblical revelation.

I hope to explain and fully answer the critics concerning the question, "Does God still speak" to people on earth? If He does, how does He communicate to human beings? Does God specifically answer? These are valid questions and I hope now to convey biblical answers without presuppositions.

The easiest and most common answer is yes, God does speak. He speaks through his Word (2 Timothy 3:16, i.e. for instruction in righteousness, Hebrews 4:12), the Holy Spirit (John 16:13), through dreams and visions (Job 33:14-15), and his eye (Psalm 32:8, 33:18, 34:15, 1 Peter 3:12). For example, when the human eye lid is down over the eye, the human being is able to see his eye. The human being may ask questions to God and He will move his eye up and down for yes and side to side for no. I have known only a few people who had this kind of relationship with God.

He also speaks after considerable effort has been made to obtain His knowledge. This is a process explained in Proverbs 2. As I understand this process, there are six steps or phases by which God reveals his knowledge.

The first step is a consistent study of God's word. You cannot short cut this spiritual journey with God. You must learn of him. This phase may take months to years to sufficiently obtain. There is not a cutoff point or an end by which you will know when you have left this phase and moved on to the next step.

Moreover, the second step is precluded by a transitional desire to value His knowledge beyond your own. You begin placing greater importance on His knowledge. You start having stronger desires to know Him through His word.

Your soul will crave the filling of the spirit of knowledge. Your heart will yearn for deeper mysteries to be revealed. The yearning satisfaction of the heart wanes after you have no more questions to be answered. Treasuring His commands includes holding on to everything He reveals as He opens your eyes to spiritual wisdom and understanding. This phase does not have a cutoff point or an end. In fact, it continues throughout your spiritual journey.

The third step is inclining your ear to wisdom. Unless you determine to live by God's word in behavior and thought, this step ends your journey. To incline means you have perked up the broadness of hearing His wisdom. The broadest range of latitude in acceptance of His wisdom requires a humble disposition of Godly fear. I believe you must have the spirit of the fear of the Lord within you to appreciate His offering of knowledge (Isaiah 11:2).

This phase is sequential in order and is manifested only after you remain in consistent study of his word and treasure his commands. Therefore the duration of time to reach this phase has no chronological age properties. You may spend years in this phase developing, considering, and applying your heart to his wisdom.

The fourth step includes searching out the scriptures to fully understand what God has revealed to you and how this impacts, changes, alters or adds to biblical data you have already understood. At this point you begin applying what He has revealed to additional knowledge, making some sense of this profound truth. It includes a larger perspective of thought and understanding of God. It further manifests deeper theological underpinnings by which what you understand opens your eyes to elementary level knowledge gained in step one.

The fifth step involves opening yourself up to the Lord confessing quite frankly you just don't understand. What He has revealed does not make sense. What He has shown you does not make sense. For what He has revealed to you does not compare to anything else you have ever seen. Your earthly wisdom is so beneath Him, so small, so finite, that what He reveals significantly lowers any concept of self.

Confessing your ignorance, asking for discernment, pleading with God to give you greater amounts of spiritual wisdom and understanding becomes the norm. To understand what He has revealed requires a mental separation distinguishing the difference of what you knew to what you now know as truth. This phase of separating the old from the new, building upon previous truth, bridging the old to the new is complex and overwhelming at times. Don't expect to speedily move through this phase.

Later on in this phase, you will come to a point where you will give up on assuming you understand everything God is revealing to you. The spiritual wisdom of God is so far excelling in knowledge, the accumulation of what I thought

I knew was a grain of sand compared to what He revealed. I have found myself daily asking God for understanding of what He revealed. So many times, I have been at a complete loss of not comprehending the slightest pretention of gain in understanding.

For example, one night while fast asleep my spirit was taken up and I saw seven spirits. My eyes were drawn to the first. As I was brought up to the spirit, I came within inches. The spirit permeated light. It was approximately two and a half inches tall and a half inch in width. I was then brought underneath the spirit. The heart of the spirit was spherical. An example of what the outer shape of the spirit resembled would be similar to a medical pill, in capsule form. The light permeated in inches from the heart of the spirit, i.e. an infinite number of light rays from the spirits heart were observed before they diminished to zero intensity. From the outer shape of the heart was approximately one and one half inches in each direction. It was comparable with the shape of a glass top chimney placed on a kerosene lamp. The height of the chimney would not have exceeded five to six inches. As you can imagine, I was in awe of seeing something so wonderful and yet had very little understanding to explain what I had just experienced.

The last step culminates in seeking and searching for God's knowledge as lost silver or hidden treasure. After God has revealed knowledge to you, your need for further explanation and sense of understanding mandates additional questions to be given to God for clarity and specificity in comprehending.

Once you know something new and it is affective to your general understanding of God's word, a curiosity develops to figure out what that means. The constant search for answers prevails in a continuous digging across domains to see knowledge as God does.

Only then will you understand the fear of the Lord and find the knowledge of God (Proverbs 2:1-5). The journey awaits, there is a beginning. He stores up sound wisdom ready to be shared if you willfully engage each phase to find the knowledge of God.

Chapter Two – The Origination of the Spirit

When a father and daughter giggle and laugh out loud, where does their emotion come from? When a couple first learns their going to have a child, where does their emotion come from? When a family experiences sadness over the death of a loved one, where does their sadness come from?

In this chapter, the human spirit is entitled the spirit of life. This is important to establish specificity of spirit in further chapters. Moreover, the very essence of spirit is described in theological terminology. The brief overview begins your search for answers concerning emotional etiology.

The essence of the spirit is eternal light (Luke 11:34-36, 24:39; John 1:4, 8:12, 9:5). According to the Christian Scriptures the spirit is separate (Job 34:14), consisting only of itself. Spirit is of God, formed by God (Zechariah 12:1) and proceeds from God (John 15:26). The Spirit is three dimensional.

This eternal life manifests intellectual properties. Individually, the spirit sees (Job 34:21; Proverbs 5:21; Jeremiah 16:17, 32:19; Hosea 7:2; Matthew 5:18, 10:26; Mark 4:22, Hebrews 4:13), keeps watch (Proverbs 15:3), runs (i.e. through the dimension of time) viewing the heart (i.e. light permeation of every human soul). The spirits remain before God's throne and speak to God, yet each sees through dimension. Collectively there are seven spirits which rejoice to see (Zechariah 4:10).

All spirit is from God and does not exist without God. Just as Jesus proceeded forth from God (John 8:42) and the Holy Spirit proceeded forth from God (John 15:26), God did not nor does He change (Hebrews 1:3, 12; 13:8; Colossians 2:9). The very thought that God never changes while His Son and Spirit proceeded forth, plus the seven spirits of God, angelic spirits, the human spirit, animal spirit (Ecclesiastics 3:22), do not lessen the constitution of God that he is unfathomable.

The Christian Scriptures state there are specific spirits which are the eyes of God. The Spirit of wisdom and understanding, the Spirit of counsel and might, and the Spirit of knowledge and fear of the Lord (Isaiah 11:2); the Spirit of God

(Genesis 1:2); the Spirit of life (Genesis 2:7); the Spirit of jealousy (Numbers 5:14); and the Spirit of holiness (Romans 1:4; Psalm 51:11).

In order for me to make sense of this phenomenon, I need to ask questions and search for those answers which build upon spiritual illumination. First, how is it possible for spirit to proceed out of God and not remove something from God? When a man and women come together and a child is conceived at that moment human life begins. A body, soul, and spirit have integrated into human life. When a male ejaculates his seed into a woman, the seed leaves the man but the man has not changed. He has remained the same. The miracle of God consummates life (Isaiah 44:3).

According to scientific study of human development, the development of a unique human individual begins with fertilization. A one-celled, fertilized egg carries all of the genetic information necessary to create an entire new organism. Only one sperm may penetrate and fertilize an ovum and determine the sex and genetic traits of a child. The genetic material of two individuals "fuses" and is translated into a new living entity called a zygote (Greek root for "yoke or join together") (Craig, Baucum, 2002).

The psycho physiological affect of conception has sequential process. Naturalism is the view that every law and every force operating in the universe is natural rather than moral, spiritual, or supernatural (MacArthur, 2003). Moreover, the affect of conception is spirit/soul/body. The physiological substance at conception does not have self-regulated properties governing the determined development. Unless you accept the DNA staircase unwinding, each cell normally divides and duplicates itself exactly. After the DNA has replicated itself, the chromosome pairs separate and reproduce the formal chromosomal arrangement of the original cell. Thus, two new cells are formed, each containing 46 chromosomes in 23 pairs just like those in the original cell (Craig, eta).

At conception, the sperm and ova meet. This union is the beginning of human life. Human life at conception is from God. The very properties that constitute mans spirit have been passed down through the act of conception without any diminishment of the spirit.

The specificity of the human soul is determinate upon Scripture (Ezekiel 18:4, 20). The Bible is the standard by which scientific theory should be evaluated. Every human being born of man is a living soul (Genesis 1:21, 2:7). Every living soul is from God. No human being has life outside of God. All human beings are children of common parents and have a common nature (Romans 5:12, 19; 1 Corinthians 15:2; Hebrews 2:16).

Has the spirit been changed throughout time? According to the Christian Scriptures, the spirit is unchanging (Job 33:4; Ecclesiastes 12:7; James 2:26), has come from God and will return to God at the moment of physiological death.

Berghash and Jillson (1998) stated the spirit wanders and it is at home wherever it is, reposes and rests in whatever it is contemplating, and is result-free and future free. The spirit is complete, it does not possess, hold, or grab, it is open to love…the spirit transcends time. Helminiak (1998) said the spirit is not sexually differentiated.

The description of the "eyes of God" (Zechariah 3:9; Revelation 5:6) is genderless. They do not possess the ability to transform themselves into a specific gender. According to Jude 6-7, spirits saw beauty and desired to have sexual relations with human beings. The only means of experiencing sexuality required the integration of spirit into the spirit of man (Genesis 6:1-2). Spirits were willing to possess the embodiment of a human being to experience sexuality.

In biblical terminology, spirits are free to will their search into the human spirit (Exodus 35:21). Each spirit sees individually without the prompting of another. Each spirit has "mind" and personality as separate from the other (2 Chronicles 16:9) spirits. The conscious, sequential process is oriented within the spirit in reciprocity of memory, free of time.

Everything a spirit sees is recorded in depth dimension in a book in heaven (Revelation 20:12; Daniel 7:10, Psalm 136:16; Hebrews 10:7). The spirits do not write in this book, moreover, what they see is recorded with time included. The recording is in three dimensions. To look at an event is to see it as real, actually taking place, in color with vocal expression and animation. The very thoughts and intents of the heart are known.

KEY TERMS

1. Conception
2. Dimension
3. Essence of Spirit
4. Eyes of God
5. Human Soul
6. Spirit

KEY QUESTIONS

1. Describe the human spirit?
2. Explain why it is important to understand the significance of the spirit?
3. How does the biblical data support or disagree with human reproduction?
4. Sometimes scientists do not include biblical data into their explanation of human development. Why is it important to include biblical data?

Quick Scripture Reference Guide

Genesis 1:2 (NKJV)

[2] The earth was without form, and void; and darkness *was* on the face of the deep. And the Spirit of God was hovering over the face of the waters.

Genesis 1:21 (NKJV)

[21] So God created great sea creatures and every living thing that moves, with which the waters abounded, according to their kind, and every winged bird according to its kind. And God saw that *it was* good.

Genesis 2:7 (NKJV)

[7] And the LORD God formed man *of* the dust of the ground, and breathed into his nostrils the breath of life; and man became a living being.

Genesis 6:1-2 (NKJV)

[1] Now it came to pass, when men began to multiply on the face of the earth, and daughters were born to them,

[2] that the sons of God saw the daughters of men, that they *were* beautiful; and they took wives for themselves of all whom they chose.

Exodus 35:21 (NKJV)

[21] Then everyone came whose heart was stirred, and everyone whose spirit was willing, *and* they brought the LORD'S offering for the work of the tabernacle of meeting, for all its service, and for the holy garments.

Numbers 5:14 (NKJV)

[14] if the spirit of jealousy comes upon him and he becomes jealous of his wife, who has defiled herself; or if the spirit of jealousy comes upon him and he becomes jealous of his wife, although she has not defiled herself—

2 Chronicles 16:9 (NKJV)

9 For the eyes of the LORD run to and fro throughout the whole earth, to show Himself strong on behalf of *those* whose heart *is* loyal to Him. In this you have done foolishly; therefore from now on you shall have wars."

Job 33:4 (NKJV)

4 The Spirit of God has made me, And the breath of the Almighty gives me life.

Job 34:14 (NKJV)

14 If He should set His heart on it, *If* He should gather to Himself His Spirit and His breath,

Job 34:21 (NKJV)

21 "For His eyes *are* on the ways of man, And He sees all his steps.

Psalm 51:11 (NKJV)

11 Do not cast me away from Your presence, And do not take Your Holy Spirit from me.

Psalm 136:16 (NKJV)

16 To Him who led His people through the wilderness, For His mercy *endures* forever;

Proverbs 5:21 (NKJV)

21 For the ways of man *are* before the eyes of the LORD, And He ponders all his paths.

Proverbs 15:3 (NKJV)

3 The eyes of the LORD *are* in every place, Keeping watch on the evil and the good.

Proverbs 20:27 (NKJV)

[27] The spirit of a man *is* the lamp of the LORD, Searching all the inner depths of his heart.

Ecclesiastes 3:22 (NKJV)

[22] So I perceived that nothing *is* better than that a man should rejoice in his own works, for that *is* his heritage. For who can bring him to see what will happen after him?

Ecclesiastes 12:7 (NKJV)

[7] Then the dust will return to the earth as it was, And the spirit will return to God who gave it.

Isaiah 11:2 (NKJV)

[2] The Spirit of the LORD shall rest upon Him, The Spirit of wisdom and understanding, The Spirit of counsel and might, The Spirit of knowledge and of the fear of the LORD.

Isaiah 38:16 (NKJV)

[16] O LORD, by these *things men* live; And in all these *things is* the life of my spirit; So You will restore me and make me live.

Isaiah 44:3 (NKJV)

[3] For I will pour water on him who is thirsty, And floods on the dry ground; I will pour My Spirit on your descendants, And My blessing on your offspring;

Jeremiah 16:17 (NKJV)

[17] For My eyes *are* on all their ways; they are not hidden from My face, nor is their iniquity hidden from My eyes.

Jeremiah 32:19 (NKJV)

[19] *You are* great in counsel and mighty in work, for your eyes *are* open to all the ways of the sons of men, to give everyone according to his ways and according to the fruit of his doings.

Ezekiel 18:4 (NKJV)

[4] "Behold, all souls are Mine; The soul of the father As well as the soul of the son is Mine; The soul who sins shall die.

Ezekiel 18:20 (NKJV)

[20] The soul who sins shall die. The son shall not bear the guilt of the father, nor the father bear the guilt of the son. The righteousness of the righteous shall be upon himself, and the wickedness of the wicked shall be upon himself.

Daniel 7:10 (NKJV)

[10] A fiery stream issued And came forth from before Him. A thousand thousands ministered to Him; Ten thousand times ten thousand stood before Him. The court was seated, And the books were opened.

Hosea 7:2 (NKJV)

[2] They do not consider in their hearts *That* I remember all their wickedness; Now their own deeds have surrounded them; They are before My face.

Zechariah 3:9 (NKJV)

[9] For behold, the stone That I have laid before Joshua: Upon the stone *are* seven eyes. Behold, I will engrave its inscription,' Says the LORD of hosts, 'And I will remove the iniquity of that land in one day.

Zechariah 4:10 (NKJV)

[10] For who has despised the day of small things? For these seven rejoice to see The plumb line in the hand of Zerubbabel. They are the eyes of the LORD, Which scan to and fro throughout the whole earth."

Zechariah 12:1 (NKJV)

[1] The burden of the word of the LORD against Israel. Thus says the LORD, who stretches out the heavens, lays the foundation of the earth, and forms the spirit of man within him:

Matthew 5:18 (NKJV)

[18] For assuredly, I say to you, till heaven and earth pass away, one jot or one tittle will by no means pass from the law till all is fulfilled.

Matthew 10:26 (NKJV)

[26] Therefore do not fear them. For there is nothing covered that will not be revealed, and hidden that will not be known.

Mark 4:22-23 (NKJV)

[22] For there is nothing hidden which will not be revealed, nor has anything been kept secret but that it should come to light.

[23] If anyone has ears to hear, let him hear."

Luke 11:34-36 (NKJV)

[34] The lamp of the body is the eye. Therefore, when your eye is good, your whole body also is full of light. But when *your eye* is bad, your body also *is* full of darkness.

[35] Therefore take heed that the light which is in you is not darkness.

[36] If then your whole body *is* full of light, having no part dark, *the* whole *body* will be full of light, as when the bright shining of a lamp gives you light."

John 8:42 (NKJV)

[42] Jesus said to them, "If God were your Father, you would love Me, for I proceeded forth and came from God; nor have I come of Myself, but He sent Me.

John 15:26 (NKJV)

26 "But when the Helper comes, whom I shall send to you from the Father, the Spirit of truth who proceeds from the Father, He will testify of Me.

Romans 1:3-4 (NKJV)

3 concerning His Son Jesus Christ our Lord, who was born of the seed of David according to the flesh,

4 *and* declared *to be* the Son of God with power according to the Spirit of holiness, by the resurrection from the dead.

Romans 5:12 (NKJV)

12 Therefore, just as through one man sin entered the world, and death through sin, and thus death spread to all men, because all sinned–

Romans 5:19 (NKJV)

19 For as by one man's disobedience many were made sinners, so also by one Man's obedience many will be made righteous.

1 Corinthians 15:1-2 (NKJV)

1 Moreover, brethren, I declare to you the gospel which I preached to you, which also you received and in which you stand,

2 by which also you are saved, if you hold fast that word which I preached to you– unless you believed in vain.

Colossians 2:9 (NKJV)

9 For in Him dwells all the fullness of the Godhead bodily;

Hebrews 1:3 (NKJV)

[3] who being the brightness of *His* glory and the express image of His person, and upholding all things by the word of His power, when He had by Himself purged our sins, sat down at the right hand of the Majesty on high,

Hebrews 1:12 (NKJV)

[12] *Like a cloak You will fold them up, And they will be changed. But You are the same, And Your years will not fail."*

Hebrews 2:16 (NKJV)

[16] For indeed He does not give aid to angels, but He does give aid to the seed of Abraham.

Hebrews 4:13 (NKJV)

[13] And there is no creature hidden from His sight, but all things *are* naked and open to the eyes of Him to whom we *must give* account.

Hebrews 10:7 (NKJV)

[7] *Then I said, 'Behold, I have come– In the volume of the book it is written of Me– To do Your will, O God.' "*

Hebrews 13:8 (NKJV)

[8] Jesus Christ *is* the same yesterday, today, and forever.

James 2:26 (NKJV)

[26] For as the body without the spirit is dead, so faith without works is dead also.

Jude 1:6-7 (NKJV)

6 And the angels who did not keep their proper domain, but left their own abode, He has reserved in everlasting chains under darkness for the judgment of the great day;

7 as Sodom and Gomorrah, and the cities around them in a similar manner to these, having given themselves over to sexual immorality and gone after strange flesh, are set forth as an example, suffering the vengeance of eternal fire.

Revelation 5:6 (NKJV)

6 And I looked, and behold, in the midst of the throne and of the four living creatures, and in the midst of the elders, stood a Lamb as though it had been slain, having seven horns and seven eyes, which are the seven Spirits of God sent out into all the earth.

Revelation 20:12 (NKJV)

12 And I saw the dead, small and great, standing before God, and books were opened. And another book was opened, which is *the Book* of Life. And the dead were judged according to their works, by the things which were written in the books.

Chapter Three – The Significance of Emotion

IN THIS CHAPTER THE ESSENCE or constitution of the spirit of life is broken down into descriptive terms. Careful attention has been given to each term and how the essence of the spirit of life is manifested. As you read this chapter, you may find the theological significance of emotions challenging your biases and presuppositions.

The etiological significance of emotion is either manifested in each spirit or within all seven as one. The seven spirits rejoice (Zechariah 4:10). Do the seven conflict causing emotion or does each as separate cause emotion? Does each spirit have emotional constructs? Are these constructs limited in stature? If so, what limitations are manifested either before God as separates, as one or in man?

"The Psychophysiology of emotion consists of affective, valenced (i.e., positive and /or negative) reactions to meaningful stimuli. Yet not all valenced reactions constitute emotions. Emotions typically are directed at particular objects. Emotions tend to be short-lived, lasting on the order of seconds to minutes" (Larsen, Bernston, Poehlmann, Ito, and Cacioppo, 2008). Some definitions describe their essence in feelings. Yet others suggest emotions are judgments. Solomon (2008) posited emotions were linked with desires, particularly self-interested, self-absorbed desires. He further sighted Descartes which defined an emotion as one type of "passion." The perceptions, feelings, or emotions of the soul…is caused by, maintained, and fortified by some movement of the spirits. Some view this as the activation by largely innate action systems, each with a particular adaptive function (Frijda, 2008).

What is the movement or the way of the spirit of life (Ecclesiastes 11:5; John 3:8)? The way of each spirit is pure, peaceable, gentle, willing to yield, full of mercy and good fruits, without partiality and without hypocrisy (James 3:17). The constitution of way is singular with definition in height and depth, moreover, pure in desire. The spirit of life manifests itself with purpose and intent. Therefore, the essence of the spirit of life is the constitution of way. That means a human being retains the spirit of life's constitution throughout their own life.

The way of spirit of life is unto the Law [Hebrew *towrah*, from *yarah*, meaning to flow as water] of God (Proverbs 13:14). Therefore, the way is fluid. The fluid is the source [Hebrew *maqowr*, meaning a source], a wellspring flowing (Proverbs 18:4). Each spirit has movement within itself. The flow of the fluid (i.e. slow, moderate, fast), remains pure all the while remaining in peace. The way of the fluid is movement of the heart.

To postulate emotion arousal as circuitry within the brain suggests only research which includes neural evidence is sufficiently unacceptable. The evidence which gives absolute specificity of emotional etiology is theological. James 3:17 describes the spirit of Life in man.

The peace of the spirit manifests constructs. It does not contest, compete, pursue, or define, yet it is always true. Singularly each spirit must always manifest its governance absent from any reactionary stimuli. Another descriptive means of manifest is the peace of the spirit remains constant. Whenever the spirit movement is greater or less it will return to its peaceable state.

As I understand this dynamic, the peace of the spirit is the regulator of emotional output. It does not control the confliction of each emotion but it does without awareness regulate the immediacy of response to still flow of the spirit (Job 32:18; Judges 13:25; Psalm 23:2) i.e. waters of rest is the same as peaceable movement of the spirit.

This explanation puts earlier theories of emotional motivation, triggering events, impulsive actions or command actions as implausible. Emotional behavior defined by motivation strongly suggested a certain prominence of urges to act, desire, or motive states (Frijda, 2008). This theory lacks theological evidence.

Another term which describes spirit is gentle. When demonic spirits initiate experience through human attachment, specific emotional characteristics emerge. In Luke 4:31-37 a man had a demonic spirit within him. The psycho-spiritual phenomena of demonic spirit within the spirit of this adult man did not change his constitution of spirit. The demonic spirit came into his spirit affecting the full manifest of spirit with in his soul. The addition of dark spirit within the spirit of man is fully separate yet within (Matthew 6:23). The dark spirit is affective within the spirit of man. It does not delineate a newness of function.

Gentle is its character. "Gentle" describes the totality of constitution, unchanging, an exact unalterable essence. When darkness (Greek *skoteeah*, means dimness, from *skotos*, meaning shadiness or shade) has come within, the spirit of life in man is unable to keep this spirit out. The spirit of life in man cannot fight for removal or determine the length of stay (John 12:35; Luke 8:26-39). Since the spirit of man is not bound by time but free from the fifth dimension, the spirit is not capable of knowing length of possession or removal date. The negative effect within is best seen through human behavior.

Since the darkness does not have moral knowledge, therefore, the eye of the spirit sees one manifestation of the essence of experience (John 3:34, Luke 11:24-26) at a time. Each spirit in the spirit of man is not in competition for experience moreover, what they see is felt experience through essence.

The emotional observable expression opposite of gentle might consist of feelings ranging from anger, anxious, defeated, defensive, disgusted, disturbed, edgy, fearful, frustration, furious, intense, irritable, malice, mean, miserable, nervous, outraged, pressured, restless, revolted, shaky, tense, terrified, uneasy, upset, uptight, or worried. The expression of emotion has etiological significance within the spirit. Therefore, the darkness of the spirit at human conception is spiritual expression and manifested as observable behavior (John 12:46).

The role of gentle emotion is expected human behavior. Infants show similar responses. A larger issue of response coincides with human development. Gentle appears to be a similar response throughout the life span. According to Scripture gentle is not genetic or environmentally influenced moreover it is spiritual expression (Luke 9:55).

Another term which describes spirit is willing to yield (James 3:17). What does it mean to have a willing spirit (Matthew 26:41; Mark 14:38; 2 Corinthians 11:4; Deuteronomy 2:30)? A willing spirit does not over power. Independent of the embodiment of flesh, the spirit singularly is willing. A willing spirit prompts to act or respond (Merriam-Webster, 2007).

Will is independent of feeling emotion (Thiessen, 1989) or regulation of emotion. This spirit prompts, moves, is ready (Proverbs 1:5,14:5, 28:8; Isa. 63:6; Dan. 4:17). Synchronization of prompting does not inflexibly influence rather, to yield the will to stronger satisfaction of the spirit's eye (Proverbs 27:20b). Moreover, willing is action ready as limited unto physiological constraints or within where control precedence is operationally bound.

Will prompts speech (Matt. 13:35), behavior (Matt. 15:32), yielding (Matt. 26:39), and process within cognition (Mark 6:25, 7:14, 58; Luke 12:18;

1 Corinthians 9:17; 12:11). It does not over power the human brain to be greater than its essence. Therefore, verbal and nonverbal emotionally expressive behaviors imbued limitation.

An example of "willing to yield" may be seen in several applications. For instance, a fifty year old man with narcissistic personality disorder has a grandiose sense of self-importance yet is able to yield his will. A thirty-eight year old woman with agoraphobia (anxiety about being in places or situations from which escape might be difficult) may have panic-like symptoms and automatically her spirit of will manifests movement to yielding calm. A twenty-eight year old man suffering from Post Traumatic Stress Disorder may re-experience recurrent and intrusive distressing recollections of an event. This adult does not remain in a hyper-vigilant state of arousal but affect of spirit moves the confliction of emotion into singularity of will.

An adolescent experiencing a preoccupation with fears of having a serious disease with elevated stress levels may have hypochondriasis yet retain the movement of a willing spirit to yield. Affectivity (i.e. the range, intensity, lability, and appropriateness of emotional response) (DSM IV, 2000) of emotion does not interfere with the essence of this spirit.

Another term which describes spirit is full of mercy and good fruits. Full (Greek *mestos*) denotes capacity, filled, occupied or complete. For the spirit to be "full of" something. Since spirit cannot be anything but spirit, only another spirit could manifest being. The Scriptures state the Spirit can be full of adultery (2 Peter 2:24), goodness (Romans 15:14), hypocrisy and iniquity (Matthew 23:28), power (Micah 3:8), and compassion (Psalm 111:4). One issue to explain, are these descriptors "adultery, goodness, hypocrisy and iniquity, power and compassion" exclusive spirits?

Describing the spirit of mercy with synonyms would include compassion, pity, clemency, forgiveness, kindness, sympathy, understanding, and leniency. Biblical examples of mercy displayed in human behavior would include pity (Psalm 103:13), compassion or yearning (Genesis 43:30), kindness (Deuteronomy 7:9), and graciousness (Psalm 4:1). Strong's Concordance of the Bible defines yearning as *kamar* – to intertwine or contract, i.e. to shrivel (as with heat).

A yearning heart is independent of biological brain function. Mercy is the manifestation of singular functionality. Singularly mercy is behavioral actions from the heart of the spirit. However, mercy is independent in substance yet intertwined with other spirits.

"Full of good fruits" is *agathos* (Greek) meaning benefit and *karpos* (Greek) meaning fruit plucked. On April 7, 2009 the Spirit to me said good fruit was sensuality. Sensuous means producing or characterized by gratification of the senses. Thus, providing pleasure through gratification of the senses for the sake of aesthetic pleasure (Merriam-Webster, 2007) for oneself (Matthew 12:35; Luke 6:45).

According to Romans 7:18-19, good, (Greek *agathos*), has no hold on brain function. The spirit is singularly sensual producing gratification of the senses. The good described is equally explanatory of Jesus (Matthew 19:16; Luke 18:19; Ephesians 1:5). The essence of good is beneficial to human life.

The spirit full of mercy and good fruits is fully occupied or complete of compassion and an ability characterized by gratification of the senses. Neither descriptors grab, make, or pressure human behavior into action. Mercy and good fruit are available, lively, and without dominion of possession.

According to the Scriptures there is not an information-processing structure of psychological mechanisms articulating procedural steps in the brain. The theory of human psychological architecture was created by, reflects, and is explained by the operation of natural selection among our ancestors is preposterous. This theory supposes selection on neural designs for functional behavior reaching out to encompass, in a network of cause and effect linkages, virtually all of human life (Tooby, Cosmides, 2008). The insidiousness of this theory is void of biblical verity. The spirit in man is not constrained by neural design.

The spirit is also without partiality and hypocrisy. Partiality (Greek *adiakritos*) means undistinguished i.e. act impartial. Unlike full of mercy and good fruits, the spirit is unable to detect lies from truth. This spirit is empty of bias. It does not detect, suspect or have suspicion. The constitution of spirit to be without partiality does not presuppose partiality exists. The spirit does not make assumptions, be biased, prejudge, or preconception of thought. To be impartial is to see without judgment. The spirit does not need to make an opinion or have an opinion. The spirit sees without benefit.

To be without hypocrisy is to never pretend. It does not hide under the appearance of another. It does not put on a false appearance. The spirit does not conceal facts, intentions, or feelings (Merriam-Webster, eta). The Greek word signifies the part taken by an actor, hence, outward show (Unger, 1988). To remain neutral of vise does not suppose what the spirit sees is good or bad. It does not judge therefore, does not qualify nor compete.

Why does man have a spirit? The Scriptures state (Genesis 1:27) "God created man in His own image." Man's entire constitution images and reflects God. God is spirit (John 4:24; Colossians 3:10; Ephesians 4:23-24). The origination of man's spirit was discussed in chapter one. Man's spirit is from God. Through the act of conception, human beings are made in the image of God – body, soul, and spirit.

Panksepp suggests a neural definition of an emotional system. Seven neural interactions are postulated to be characteristics of all major primary-process emotional systems of the brain. The important criterion that emotional systems… assumed that arousal of the whole executive circuitry for each emotion is essential for elaborating emotional feeling within the brain, perhaps by interacting with other subneocortical brain circuits for organismic visceral self-representation (Panksepp, 2008). Emotion is not a system of arousal but an expression of the spirit. In fact it is the confliction of movement of the spirits within the spirit of each human being.

The significance of emotion in man is the spirit in man constitutes emotion in man. Through the movement of the spirit in man, behavioral expression is recognizable and categorization of emotion is made.

In Psalm 36:8 David described God gives people drink (Hebrew *shaqah*, meaning to cause to irrigate or furnish a potion to *drink*) from the river (Hebrew *nachalah*, meaning a stream) of your pleasures (Hebrew *ednah*, from to the root word *adan*, meaning to be soft or pleasant which means pleasure). God gives each human being a spirit at conception which is fluid. That fluid is the source of human passion, emotion, and feeling. He causes all human beings to experience pleasure. Therefore, neural activity does not create affective experience as Pankseff (Panksepp, 2008) hypothesized.

In Psalm 46:4 Korah described the river in the holy place of the tabernacle of God. He said there is a river (Hebrew *nahar*, meaning a stream) whose streams (Hebrew *peleg*, from *palag*, meaning to split means a rill, i.e. small channel of water) make glad (Hebrew *sameach*, from *samach*, meaning to cause to make blithe or gleeful i.e. glad, joyful, pleasure) the city (Hebrew *ir*, from *uwr*, to wake, through the idea of opening the eyes, meaning city) of God. According to this scripture it is the river i.e. fluid, which makes people glad. There is a literal river in the city of God which is spirit (Revelation 22:1). It flows throughout the city of God. The very essence of spirit in each human being is fluid from God. The spirit is causal of emotional arousal and through physiological substance each human being has emotional affect.

Panksepp (2008) said "to the best of our knowledge, raw emotional feelings arise from ancient pre-propositional subneocortical substrates that are homologous in all mammals." A principle central to the affective neuroscience view of basic feelings states "homeostatic feelings 'emotions', clearly these affective states correspond to arousals of the primitive brain areas that animal research has revealed as critically important for generating the instinctual behaviors associated with those bodily drives." I disagree completely with this principle. The brain does not generate arousal. Arousal is generated from the spirit in man.

KEY TERMS

1. Arousal
2. Emotion
3. Emotional observable expression
4. Full of mercy and good fruits
5. Gentle
6. Peace of the Spirit
7. Significance of Spirit
8. Willing to yield
9. Without partiality and hypocrisy

KEY QUESTIONS

1. What is the significance of having a spirit?
2. Explain the way of the spirit?
3. How does the peace of the spirit affect human emotion?
4. What are the differences between the peace of the spirit and gentle of spirit?
5. Sometimes a person may regulate their emotions, how does willing to yield prompt human behavior?
6. When is behavioral expression recognizable in emotion?

Quick Scripture Reference Guide

Genesis 1:27 (NKJV)

27 So God created man in His *own* image; in the image of God He created him;
male and female He created them.

Genesis 43:30 (NKJV)

30 Now his heart yearned for his brother; so Joseph made haste and sought *some-where* to weep. And he went into *his* chamber and wept there.

Deuteronomy 2:30 (NKJV)

30 But Sihon king of Heshbon would not let us pass through, for the LORD your God hardened his spirit and made his heart obstinate, that He might deliver him into your hand, as *it is* this day.

Deuteronomy 7:9 (NKJV)

9 Therefore know that the LORD your God, He *is* God, the faithful God who keeps covenant and mercy for a thousand generations with those who love Him and keep His commandments;

Judges 13:25 (NKJV)

25 And the Spirit of the LORD began to move upon him at Mahaneh Dan between Zorah and Eshtaol.

Job 32:8 (NKJV)

8 But *there is* a spirit in man, And the breath of the Almighty gives him understanding.

Job 32:18 (NKJV)

18 For I am full of words; The spirit within me compels me.

Psalm 4:1 (NKJV)

[1] To the Chief Musician. With stringed instruments. A Psalm of David. Hear me when I call, O God of my righteousness! You have relieved me in *my* distress; Have mercy on me, and hear my prayer.

Psalm 23:2 (NKJV)

[2] He makes me to lie down in green pastures; He leads me beside the still waters.

Psalm 36:8 (NKJV)

[8] They are abundantly satisfied with the fullness of Your house, And You give them drink from the river of Your pleasures.

Psalm 46:4 (NKJV)

[4] *There is* a river whose streams shall make glad the city of God, The holy *place* of the tabernacle of the Most High.

Psalm 103:13 (NKJV)

[13] As a father pities *his* children, *So* the LORD pities those who fear Him.

Psalm 111:4 (NKJV)

[4] He has made His wonderful works to be remembered; The LORD *is* gracious and full of compassion.

Proverbs 1:5 (NKJV)

[5] A wise *man* will hear and increase learning, And a man of understanding will attain wise counsel,

Proverbs 13:14 (NKJV)

[14] The law of the wise *is* a fountain of life, To turn *one* away from the snares of death.

Proverbs 14:5 (NKJV)

[5] A faithful witness does not lie, But a false witness will utter lies.

Proverbs 17:27 (NKJV)

[27] He who has knowledge spares his words, *And* a man of understanding is of a calm spirit.

Proverbs 18:4 (NKJV)

[4] The words of a man's mouth *are* deep waters; The wellspring of wisdom *is* a flowing brook.

Proverbs 27:20 (NKJV)

[20] Hell and Destruction are never full; So the eyes of man are never satisfied.

Proverbs 28:8 (NKJV)

[8] One who increases his possessions by usury and extortion Gathers it for him who will pity the poor.

Isaiah 63:6 (NKJV)

[6] I have trodden down the peoples in My anger, Made them drunk in My fury, And brought down their strength to the earth."

Ecclesiastes 11:5 (NKJV)

[5] As you do not know what *is* the way of the wind, *Or* how the bones *grow* in the womb of her who is with child, So you do not know the works of God who makes everything.

Daniel 4:17 (NKJV)

[17] 'This decision *is* by the decree of the watchers, And the sentence by the word of the holy ones, In order that the living may know That the Most High rules in the kingdom of men, Gives it to whomever He will, And sets over it the lowest of men.'

Micah 3:8 (NKJV)

8 But truly I am full of power by the Spirit of the LORD, And of justice and might, To declare to Jacob his transgression And to Israel his sin.

Zechariah 4:10 (NKJV)

10 For who has despised the day of small things? For these seven rejoice to see The plumb line in the hand of Zerubbabel. They are the eyes of the LORD, Which scan to and fro throughout the whole earth."

Matthew 6:23 (NKJV)

23 But if your eye is bad, your whole body will be full of darkness. If therefore the light that is in you is darkness, how great *is* that darkness!

Matthew 12:35 (NKJV)

35 A good man out of the good treasure of his heart brings forth good things, and an evil man out of the evil treasure brings forth evil things.

Matthew 13:35 (NKJV)

35 that it might be fulfilled which was spoken by the prophet, saying: *"I will open My mouth in parables; I will utter things kept secret from the foundation of the world."*

Matthew 15:32 (NKJV)

32 Now Jesus called His disciples to *Himself* and said, "I have compassion on the multitude, because they have now continued with Me three days and have nothing to eat. And I do not want to send them away hungry, lest they faint on the way."

Matthew 19:16 (NKJV)

16 Now behold, one came and said to Him, "Good Teacher, what good thing shall I do that I may have eternal life?"

Matthew 23:28 (NKJV)

28 Even so you also outwardly appear righteous to men, but inside you are full of hypocrisy and lawlessness.

Matthew 26:39 (NKJV)

39 He went a little farther and fell on His face, and prayed, saying, "O My Father, if it is possible, let this cup pass from Me; nevertheless, not as I will, but as You *will.*"

Matthew 26:41 (NKJV)

41 Watch and pray, lest you enter into temptation. The spirit indeed *is* willing, but the flesh *is* weak."

Mark 6:25 (NKJV)

25 Immediately she came in with haste to the king and asked, saying, "I want you to give me at once the head of John the Baptist on a platter."

Mark 7:14 (NKJV)

14 When He had called all the multitude to *Himself,* He said to them, "Hear Me, everyone, and understand:

Mark 14:38 (NKJV)

38 Watch and pray, lest you enter into temptation. The spirit indeed *is* willing, but the flesh *is* weak."

Luke 4:31-37 (NKJV)

31 Then He went down to Capernaum, a city of Galilee, and was teaching them on the Sabbaths.

32 And they were astonished at His teaching, for His word was with authority.

33 Now in the synagogue there was a man who had a spirit of an unclean demon. And he cried out with a loud voice,

34 saying, "Let *us* alone! What have we to do with You, Jesus of Nazareth? Did You come to destroy us? I know who You are–the Holy One of God!"

35 But Jesus rebuked him, saying, "Be quiet, and come out of him!" And when the demon had thrown him in *their* midst, it came out of him and did not hurt him.

36 Then they were all amazed and spoke among themselves, saying, "What a word this *is!* For with authority and power He commands the unclean spirits, and they come out."

37 And the report about Him went out into every place in the surrounding region.

Luke 6:45 (NKJV)

45 A good man out of the good treasure of his heart brings forth good; and an evil man out of the evil treasure of his heart brings forth evil. For out of the abundance of the heart his mouth speaks.

Luke 8:26-39 (NKJV)

26 Then they sailed to the country of the Gadarenes, which is opposite Galilee.

27 And when He stepped out on the land, there met Him a certain man from the city who had demons for a long time. And he wore no clothes, nor did he live in a house but in the tombs.

28 When he saw Jesus, he cried out, fell down before Him, and with a loud voice said, "What have I to do with You, Jesus, Son of the Most High God? I beg You, do not torment me!"

29 For He had commanded the unclean spirit to come out of the man. For it had often seized him, and he was kept under guard, bound with chains and shackles; and he broke the bonds and was driven by the demon into the wilderness.

30 Jesus asked him, saying, "What is your name?" And he said, "Legion," because many demons had entered him.

31 And they begged Him that He would not command them to go out into the abyss.

32 Now a herd of many swine was feeding there on the mountain. So they begged Him that He would permit them to enter them. And He permitted them.

33 Then the demons went out of the man and entered the swine, and the herd ran violently down the steep place into the lake and drowned.

34 When those who fed *them* saw what had happened, they fled and told *it* in the city and in the country.

35 Then they went out to see what had happened, and came to Jesus, and found the man from whom the demons had departed, sitting at the feet of Jesus, clothed and in his right mind. And they were afraid.

36 They also who had seen *it* told them by what means he who had been demon-possessed was healed.

37 Then the whole multitude of the surrounding region of the Gadarenes asked Him to depart from them, for they were seized with great fear. And He got into the boat and returned.

38 Now the man from whom the demons had departed begged Him that he might be with Him. But Jesus sent him away, saying,

39 "Return to your own house, and tell what great things God has done for you." And he went his way and proclaimed throughout the whole city what great things Jesus had done for him.

Luke 9:55 (NKJV)

55 But He turned and rebuked them, and said, "You do not know what manner of spirit you are of.

Luke 11:24-26 (NKJV)

24 "When an unclean spirit goes out of a man, he goes through dry places, seeking rest; and finding none, he says, 'I will return to my house from which I came.'

25 And when he comes, he finds *it* swept and put in order.

[26] Then he goes and takes with *him* seven other spirits more wicked than himself, and they enter and dwell there; and the last *state* of that man is worse than the first."

Luke 12:18 (NKJV)

[18] So he said, 'I will do this: I will pull down my barns and build greater, and there I will store all my crops and my goods.

Luke 18:19 (NKJV)

[19] So Jesus said to him, "Why do you call Me good? No one *is* good but One, *that is,* God.

John 3:8 (NKJV)

[8] The wind blows where it wishes, and you hear the sound of it, but cannot tell where it comes from and where it goes. So is everyone who is born of the Spirit."

John 3:34 (NKJV)

[34] For He whom God has sent speaks the words of God, for God does not give the Spirit by measure.

John 4:24 (NKJV)

[24] God *is* Spirit, and those who worship Him must worship in spirit and truth."

John 12:35 (NKJV)

[35] Then Jesus said to them, "A little while longer the light is with you. Walk while you have the light, lest darkness overtake you; he who walks in darkness does not know where he is going.

John 12:46 (NKJV)

[46] I have come *as* a light into the world, that whoever believes in Me should not abide in darkness.

Romans 7:18-19 (NKJV)

[18] For I know that in me (that is, in my flesh) nothing good dwells; for to will is present with me, but *how* to perform what is good I do not find.

[19] For the good that I will *to do,* I do not do; but the evil I will not *to do,* that I practice.

Romans 15:14 (NKJV)

[14] Now I myself am confident concerning you, my brethren, that you also are full of goodness, filled with all knowledge, able also to admonish one another.

1 Corinthians 9:17 (NKJV)

[17] For if I do this willingly, I have a reward; but if against my will, I have been entrusted with a stewardship.

1 Corinthians 12:11 (NKJV)

[11] But one and the same Spirit works all these things, distributing to each one individually as He wills.

2 Corinthians 11:4 (NKJV)

[4] For if he who comes preaches another Jesus whom we have not preached, or *if* you receive a different spirit which you have not received, or a different gospel which you have not accepted–you may well put up with it!

Ephesians 1:5 (NKJV)

[5] having predestined us to adoption as sons by Jesus Christ to Himself, according to the good pleasure of His will,

Ephesians 4:23-24 (NKJV)

[23] and be renewed in the spirit of your mind,

[24] and that you put on the new man which was created according to God, in true righteousness and holiness.

Colossians 3:10 (NKJV)

[10] and have put on the new *man* who is renewed in knowledge according to the image of Him who created him,

James 3:17 (NKJV)

[17] But the wisdom that is from above is first pure, then peaceable, gentle, willing to yield, full of mercy and good fruits, without partiality and without hypocrisy.

2 Peter 2:14 (NKJV)

[14] having eyes full of adultery and that cannot cease from sin, enticing unstable souls. *They have* a heart trained in covetous practices, *and are* accursed children.

Revelation 22:1 (NKJV)

[1] And he showed me a pure river of water of life, clear as crystal, proceeding from the throne of God and of the Lamb.

Chapter Four – Emotional Change and Impact

CHARTING THE FREQUENCY A SPIRIT comes or leaves a human being is difficult unless observation of behavior is examined. To know exactly when a spirit comes and leaves is not observable. Moreover, when a spirit comes, a human being does have immediate effectual characteristics. There is not a vast field of biblical research to explain the phenomenon. So in this chapter the focus will be on coming and going of a spirit from a human being and the subsequent impact.

Only one spirit has optical sight through the spirit of life at a time. Optical sight is "seeing" through the eye of the spirit of life. What the spirit sees is the feeling, process of cognition, and behavior as experienced in a human being. Another way of saying this is the spirit sees me as experiencing the intensified emotion.

Even though a spirit is in the spirit of life it does not move to affect human behavior within until it has optical sight. The spirit of life has one eye. Each spirit inside is true to its essence. Moreover, the effective observable human behavior is constrained to the spirit "seeing". The spirit determines the what, how and the way you "see" life.

Sterns (2008) states emotional standards – the "feeling rules" or emotionology - describes socially prescribed emotional values as criteria to evaluate emotional experience. Causality of emotions is not human rule or socially prescribed, but essence of spirit within the spirit of life of a human being. The social constructs of emotionality are not value driven. Therefore, emotions are not biologically predetermined. The bio-physiological human self cannot cause emotion nor have preconditions of emotion. Without the spirit the bio-physical human self is void of emotional causality.

In the Old Testament, God's spirit would come upon human beings and leave. There was not a permanent indwelling within the spirit of life (Exodus 31:3; 35:31; Numbers 24:2, 27:18; Judges 3:10, 6:34; 11:29; 14:6, 19; 15:14, 19; 1 Samuel 10:6, 10; 11:6; 16:13; 1 Kings 22:21; 1 Chronicles 12:18; 2 Chronicles 15:1; 20:14; Job 26:4). A variety of emotions were behaviorally evident when the spirit came upon human beings. Usually God forewarned his servant of the change that was coming. When His spirit came and they began to do as God said, each one would know he had received another spirit from God.

The affect of a new spirit is governed and controlled by God. His sovereignty over all spirits and human beings began prior to three dimensional (height, width, length) integration. In Daniel 4:35, God sovereignly does His will in His created spirits and in all human beings (Psalm 115:3; 22:28; 1 Timothy 6:15).

The historical contribution of emotional change as instrumentally guided, directed, and controlled is absolute, irresistible, and infinite. God is personally involved in the affairs of every human being. He instigates change in every human being. Human beings are not mere puppets awaiting a pull of a string. Moreover, we are subject to the essence of every spirit sent by God whereby orchestrating change and its impact.

Historically, psycho dynamic historians emphasized the conscious actions and rational decisions in the "Middle Ages". Accusations emerged as ordinary people were described as impulsiveness and stressed transcendent rationality. During the 1960's, a Freudian theoretical framework concentrated on biography and linked emotional characteristics to historical developments, i.e. harsh father with a preoccupation of an angry and omnipotent God, emerged (Stearns, 2008).

By the 1970's, emotional patterns were central to the task that produced increasing confluence with other disciplines dealing with the social contexts of emotional life. By the 20th century, a redefinition of fear emerged focusing on inward demons. The emotional spontaneity generated new measures designed to curb spontaneity (Sterns, eta). Unfortunately, theological writing was not included and psychodynamic research exploded leading new trends of empirical findings. This absence has broadened research to observational study and theoretical work.

According to Job 32:8, every human being does have a spirit, i.e. the spirit of life. The spirit is the heart of human emotions. Without the spirit in man, man would not have life. The adding of spirits that come into the spirit of life is affective. The brighter the light of the spirit is equal to the greater emotional output. No human being is void of spirit.

The light of the eye rejoices the heart (Proverbs 15:30). The light of the eye of the spirit "comes out" of the spirits eye and rejoices the heart. It rejoices the heart, i.e. the core of spirit, for the light to come out of the eye. This is the means of expression of spirit. It is also the means by which human beings are expressive, i.e. bio/physiological substance is dependent upon the spirit for emotion.

The Spirit of the Lord also departs from the human spirit (1 Samuel 16:14, 23; 2 Kings 2:16; 2 Chronicles 9:4; 2 Chronicles 18:20, 23; Ezra 1:5). The ability of departure is sovereign determination not self or spirit determination. When the spirits work is fulfilled, it leaves the human spirit having completed its appointed task.

One example of this would be when a human being commits murder his emotional outrage has low regulation with high motive impulse. Immediately after the act is completed this spirit leaves and the human being becomes calm. Although human feelings of regret, guilt, or shame may emerge, the willful completion of murder is satisfied. The spirit has fulfilled its task and returned leaving his spirit void of any threatening behavior. Samson is a good example of this phenomenon.

Another example illustrates the departing of one spirit and immediately another spirit comes. In 1 Samuel 16:14-23, the spirit of the Lord departs (Hebrew *sur,* meaning to turn off) from Saul and immediately a distressing i.e. evil (Hebrew *rah*, means bad [Hebrew *raa,* meaning to spoil]) spirit from the Lord troubles (Hebrew *baat*, means to fear) Saul.

Immediately Saul became afraid. He was troubled or terrified. Samuel did not make Saul afraid, the spirit made him afraid. The Spirit caused him to fear. The emotional display of arousal is caused by this distressing spirit. The movement of this spirit within his spirit caused the cognitive behavioral changes in Saul. The research which suggests fear acquisition from neural circuitry conditioning is speculative.

Ledoux and Phelps (2008) found the retention of an abstract, cognitive representation of fear may depend on the hippocampus. Functional magnetic resonance imaging shows enhanced activation in the left amygdale to a "threat" stimulus. Humans can acquire fears through social means, including instruction and observation.

They also suggest human beings can regulate their own fears based on animal models of extinction learning. Recent anatomical MRI study demonstrated that the relative cortical size of the region predicts the rate of extinction learning across individuals. Recent studies have explored the neural mechanisms to alter fear responses. It is thought that emotional regulation underlies higher cognitive functions such as executive control.

Until the differences of spirit are defined and articulated research will continue to study brain origination for emotional regulation. This handbook begins to refocus etiological foundations for emotion, its cause, regulation, and confliction. Recent studies have not included theological wisdom whereby mishandling theoretic frameworks.

Samuel (1 Samuel 16:23) noticed when the spirit from God was upon Saul, that David was affected by the spirit. David played a harp with his hand. Saul would not have seen the spirit come to David, nor would he be able to see the spirit come to him. However, he did notice a change in David and himself. David was moved by the spirit to play the harp. His cognitive interest was in playing the harp. Saul said he would become refreshed (Hebrew *rawah*, means to breathe) and well (Hebrew *tob*, means to be or make good) and the distressing (Hebrew *ra*, meaning bad) spirit would depart (Hebrew *sur*, means to turn off) from him.

The effect of the spirit coming into David caused mobility in David. For example, he would go and get the harp. The spirit moved David to go and get the harp. Then to further move David to play the harp so that the music would be pleasing to Saul. The Hebrew language does not suggest the spirit that moved Saul and David was evil. In fact, the usage of the word spirit does not specify exactly. If this was the distressing spirit from verse 14-15, then it was evil. Moreover, it was still from God.

The distressing spirit had affective purpose to Saul. His emotional disposition changed whenever the distressing spirit came upon him. God uses evil spirits in the dark kingdom and good spirits to affect the lives of people on earth. Saul turned his back on God from following him and did not perform his commandments (1 Samuel 15:11). Therefore, God sent an evil spirit which affected Saul emotionally, and intellectually.

When the distressing spirit had completed its assignment, the spirit left Saul. Saul was returning after a war and some women came out singing "Saul has slain his thousands, and David his ten thousands." Saul became very angry. The next day, the distressing spirit returned to Saul, Saul prophesied and David played a harp again. Saul took the spear in his hand and threw it at David (1 Samuel 18:1-16).

Saul was unable to regulate his emotions. His anger grew stronger and his jealousy over David motivated his selfish desires. This spirit moved Saul to higher levels of anger and jealousy. Without the distressing spirit, Saul would not have felt threatened. Saul was unable to control his feelings and his anger grew to malice. He had exceeded his threshold to regulate his feelings. Instead of yelling, stomping, crying, or screaming at David, he threw a spear to hurt David.

The spirit in Saul affected his cognitive development reversing his logical solution based thinking to a preoperational thinking which is more descriptive of children age two to seven. Saul was not thinking about cause and effect. What would happen to him if he threw the spear at David? How would the relationship change? The impact of one spirit had affect on Saul's emotions and cognition.

Saul once again knew he had to kill David. Saul's anger was moving him to strike David (1 Samuel 19:1-10). After another war was concluded, Saul was back in his house and David was playing music again. God sent the same distressing spirit back to Saul to once again try to kill David. Saul, still unable to regulate his emotions, was moved to throw his spear at David again.

Notice the distressed spirit moved upon Saul through his emotions. Saul's emotions became conflictual whereby his physiological self could not regulate or hold back the intensity within his heart. Saul was moved by the evil spirit, causing distress within Saul's heart. Anger, jealously, hatred, envy, and spite, now seen as aggressive behavior, became intensified whereby Saul could not regulate his own feelings.

I would like to try and explain how this is possible. How does the spirit move within the spirit of life of every human being to affect human control and regulation? In Ezekiel 3:14 "so the spirit lifted me up, and took me away, and I went in bitterness (Hebrew *bara*, meaning bitter), in the heat (Hebrew *hema*, meaning heat) of my spirit; but the hand of the LORD was strong upon me."

Ezekiel was moved within his heart. His heart is the core of the spirit of life within him. The core of the heart is eternal light. The light glows in intensity which moves the human being as his emotions are now conflicted. The addition of spirit within the core of the heart is a change in self concept and the lack of regulation of emotional intensity becomes observable through behavior.

The emotion, bitterness, is not a neurophysiological affect. Wager, Barrett, Bliss-Moreau, Lindquist, Duncan, Kober, Joseph, Davidson, and Mize (2008) theorized animal models provide exquisite neurophysiological detail that constrains theories about mental processes, and neuropsychology provides unique evidence on the brain components necessary for intact emotional processes in humans. I disagree with this hypothesis completely.

The scriptures states the etiological beginning starts in the heart (Ezekiel 27:31; Proverbs 14:10). Bitterness does not begin in the human brain. Neuroimaging may show the effect of the spirit which produces bitterness and is evident in the brain, i.e. midbrain periaqueductal gray (PAG), which is thought to coordinate coherent physiological and behavioral responses to threat (Wager, et.al). However, it does not begin in biological physiological substance. All emotion has its beginning in the core of the heart.

Proverbs 15:4 states the wrenching of the spirit distorts the pure essence of the spirit. "A wholesome tongue *is* a tree of life: but perverseness (Hebrew *selep*, means to distort, from the Hebrew word *salap,* meaning to wrench) therein *is* a breach (Hebrew *sheber,* meaning a fracture from the Hebrew word *shabar,* meaning to burst) in the spirit." Notice the wrenching of the spirit takes place inside the core of the spirit. Wrenching or turning from its pure essence within cause distortions. The distortions are in conflict with its pure essence and causes emotional intensity. If the purpose of the spirit is to over stimulate the human being with intense distortion, regulation of emotion will not be possible.

To illustrate the over stimulative ability of the spirit, Samson is a good example of reference. In Judges 13:25, "And the Spirit of the LORD began to move him at times in the camp of Dan between Zorah and Eshtaol." The spirit caused Samson to "move" (Hebrew *paam,* meaning to tap or impel, from Hebrew *Halal,* meaning to bore, from Hebrew *hil,* meaning to twist or whirl). The spirit urged or drove Samson forward, twisting his felt emotions. One negative emotion which is descriptive of this is impulsivity.

Impulsivity is a low constraint (force to hold back) and negative emotionality. Chapple and Johnson (2007) state this is an inability to defer gratification and curb impulses and anger. Their research results showed the paths between discipline and impulsivity, and maternal attachment and impulsivity differed significantly for boys and girls. They posited it is not the greater amount of control exerted by families on girls that produces a gender differentiated path to impulsivity, but rather that boys' less constrained familial environments differentially increases their impulsivity.

Samson was impulsive when he saw a woman he wanted in Timnah. Samson became angry with his father and told him to "get her for me, for she pleases me." Later, the spirit came upon him again and he grabbed a roaring lion and tore it apart. Then on his way back home, he found the torn lion and ate some of the honey in the carcass of the lion. The cause of his impulsivity was the twisting of his felt emotions. The spirit moved him by impelling him.

Consider another man who was impulsive yet targeted his nervousness and fear in a less constrained manner. In Deuteronomy 2:26-31 (KJV), Moses said "And I sent messengers out of the wilderness of Kedemoth unto Sihon king of Heshbon with words of peace, saying, Let me pass through thy land: I will go along by the high way, I will neither turn unto the right hand nor to the left. Thou shalt sell me meat for money, that I may eat; and give me water for money, that I may drink: only I will pass through on my feet; (As the children of Esau which dwell in Seir, and the Moabites which dwell in Ar, did unto me;) until I shall pass over Jordan into the land which the LORD our God giveth us. But Sihon king of Heshbon would not let us pass by him: for the LORD thy God hardened his spirit, and made his heart obstinate, that he might deliver him into thy hand, as *appeareth* this day. And the LORD said unto me, Behold, I have begun to give Sihon and his land before thee: begin to possess, that thou mayest inherit his land."

King Sihon's heart was hardened (Hebrew *quasha*, meaning to be dense) his spirit, and made (Hebrew *lebab*, meaning the heart, taken from the Hebrew word *labab,* meaning to enclose) his heart obstinate (Hebrew *amesm,* meaning to be alert). God made King Sihon's heart dense. He would not let Israel pass through his land. What could have been a nice gesture on the King's part, instead, he could not see the benefit of letting Israel pass through his land (Numbers 21:23).

In turn, God told Moses he had begun to give Sihon and his land over to Israel to possess and inherit the land. Soon Israel defeated King Sihon and his men and women and kept only the livestock. Notice how involved God was in hardening King Sihon's spirit. This hardening eventually brought about the death of the King.

How intensified was the level of emotion as designed by God through making King Sihon's heart dense? How dense does the core of the spirit have to become to observe this kind of behavior? What happened to his spirit?

For God to make King Sihon's heart alerted with intensified fear or anger is one thing. To move a whole city of people to be that afraid or angry at Israel could have been done by one spirit is quite another. To harden a spirit is to thicken the fluidity of mobility of the spirit. The affect of slow mobility increases intensity of fluidity (Deuteronomy 2:30).

The intensity of fluidity does not suggest each human being controls their emotional output. Theologically, the spirit mobility is regulated by the individual spirit and not human control. King Sihon could only behave as the spirit within him impelled him.

Here is another example of spirit impelling human action. In Job 32:16-22 (NKJV) "And I have waited, because they did not speak, because they stood still *and* answered no more. I also will answer my part, I too will declare my opinion. For I am full of words; the spirit within me compels me. Indeed my belly *is* like wine *that* has no vent; It is ready to burst like new wineskins. I will speak, that I may find relief; I must open my lips and answer. Let me not, I pray, show partiality to anyone; Nor let me flatter any man. For I do not know how to flatter, *Else* my Maker would soon take me away".

Elihu waited to speak to Job. His three friends had already questioned him extensively. After they had angrily spoken to Job and had apparently finished their accusations, Elihu began to speak. Notice he wanted to say something throughout this dialog, but he did not. He did not give his advice or counsel to Job when his three friends were already questioning him. Elihu said he was full (Hebrew *mala*, meaning to fill) of matter (Hebrew *milla,* from the Hebrew word *malal*, meaning to speak). He had a lot to say to Job.

Elihu said the spirit within me compels (Hebrew *suq,* meaning to suppress) me. The spirit in him kept him from talking. The spirit regulated his cognition process and impulsiveness by slowly moving him. His emotional release was subjected to time. His friends had to speak first before he was allowed to speak. If Elihu regulated himself then his substrates within his neuronal circuitry i.e. localized electrical stimulations of specific neural systems (LESSONS), controlled his emotional and cognitive expression as Panksepp (2008) has suggested. However, this is not the case.

Time is a dimension (dimension 5) integrated within height, width and depth. Spirits travel in and out of time. They are not submissive to time nor do they regulate it. The spirit suppressed Elihu from talking in order to control his behavior. The Scriptures validate this phenomenon. Notice the level of anguish within Elihu for not being able to talk. He wanted relief and needed to talk to gain the relief from holding in his thoughts and feelings.

The spirit in Elihu gradually moved within him. Other spirits within his spirit of life show no partiality of superiority. They are not in competition. To understand Elihu's behavior is to see the fluidity of movement of his spirit. Elihu could not behave in any manner over which his spirit had not moved him to behave. The buildup of emotional pressure caused the eventual release of cognitive thought.

Another example of this phenomenon is through Job himself (Job 6:1-7 TEV). "If my troubles and grief's were weighed on scales, they would weigh more than the sands of the sea, so my wild words should not surprise you. Almighty God has shot me with arrows, and their poison spreads through my body. God has lined up his terrors against me. A donkey is content when eating grass, and a cow is quiet when eating hay. But who can eat flat, unsalted food? What taste is there in the white of an egg? I have no appetite for food like that, and everything I eat makes me sick."

In this case, Job's physical appetite was affected by his spirit. Although he blamed his depression upon God, his spirit caused his biological and psychological maladjustment. Notice it was not environmental influence which had etiological properties, but the spirit within his spirit of life that had effect.

For the arrows (Hebrew *hes,* meaning a piercer from Hebrew *hasas,* meaning to chop into, to pierce) of the Almighty, are within me, the poison (Hebrew *hema,* meaning heat, from Hebrew *yaham,* means to be hot, i.e. anger) drinks (Hebrew *shata,* meaning to imbibe, i.e. to soak, to receive into the mind and retain) up my spirit.

Notice what happened. God made his spirit to be in multiple. So that Job would become angry over many things that his friend Eliphaz had said to him.

His anger levels continued to raise meanwhile his spirit continued to elevate the anger. Job became so angry that he would not eat.

To suggest he could not regulate his anger on his own and talk himself through his friend's advice would inaccurately portray Job as consciously in control of his emotions. If this were true then human behavior would be regulatory. If untrue as the scriptures state, then the determined human behavior is the outcome of the fluidity of the spirit within the spirit of life in each human being. Jobs anger was from the spirit which permeates the spirit of life. The spirit of life has mind and the eye to "see". This spirit moved Job to feel physiologically sick. Therefore, he would not eat certain foods.

Jeremiah stated the spirit is affective in human cognition. In 2 Chronicles 36:22 (see Ezra 1:1; 1 Chronicles 5:26), "Now in the first year of Cyrus king of Persia, that the word of the LORD *spoken* by the mouth of Jeremiah might be accomplished, the LORD stirred up the spirit of Cyrus king of Persia, that he made a proclamation throughout all his kingdom, and *put it* also in writing, saying, Thus saith Cyrus king of Persia, All the kingdoms of the earth hath the LORD God of heaven given me; and he hath charged me to build him an house in Jerusalem, which *is* in Judah. Who *is there* among you of all his people? The LORD his God *be* with him, and let him go up."

In order that the word of the LORD be accomplished, the LORD stirred (Hebrew *ur,* meaning to wake, to be bare. It has the idea of opening the eyes or through the eyes) up the spirit of Cyrus…that he made a proclamation. In a chronological sense, the eye of the spirit of life is open and those spirits within look out. When they look out through the spirit of life eye, i.e. one at a time, the spirit sees what the human being will do, and it returns down within the heart of the spirit to accomplish its given task.

This corresponds to what Jesus said in Mark 7: 21-23. "For from within, out of the heart of men, proceed evil thoughts, adulteries, fornications, murders, thefts, covetousness, wickedness, deceit, lewdness, an evil eye, blasphemy, pride, foolishness. All these evil things come from within and defile a man."

You might be thinking since God makes his spirits do very specific things within our spirit of life, how can each person be responsible to employ moral rationale. The answer rests in scripture. Since Adam sinned in the garden, God determined all his seed would have his nature. Man's new nature is fully affected by sin (Romans 5:12-21; Genesis 2:17). Spirits accomplish the sovereign plan of God for all human beings. God does not mediate our sinful behavior, human beings are already sinful. Because human beings are sinful, God's spirits employ the restricted fluid move-ability which exemplifies man's nature under God's law.

There is one other text that is descriptive of impact and change. Pharaoh's spirit was troubled, evidently, by a dream he had that night (Genesis 41:8; Job 21:4; Psalm 77:3, 142:3, 143:4; Daniel 2:1, 3; 4). His troubled (Hebrew *pa'am,* meaning to tap i.e. beat regularly, in general to impel) spirit moved him to send for his magicians of Egypt. Notice he was not moved to summon his magician's right after his dreams, but after his spirit moved his heart to be troubled.

The stress and anxiety Pharaoh suffered from was not biologically/physiologically induced. The spirit caused his heart to be troubled and thereby impelled him to call his magicians. The etiological affect of emotional impact and change in human behavior is effectual through the spirit of life.

KEY TERMS

1. Bitterness
2. Concrete operational thinking
3. Effect of the spirit
4. Emotional disposition
5. Emotionology
6. Harden a spirit
7. Heart
8. Impulsivity
9. Optical sight
10. Spirit determination
11. Wrenching of the spirit

KEY QUESTIONS

1. What does a spirit "see" in each human being?
2. Why must a spirit "see" to effect human behavior?
3. How is a spirit controlled in each human being?
4. How does a spirit regulate human emotion?
5. What causes a human being to feel distress?
6. Where does a spirit move to affect a human being?
7. Where is the etiological beginning of human emotion?
8. Who hardens the heart of every human being?
9. Why is the spirit affective in human cognition?

Quick Scripture Reference Guide

Genesis 2:17 (NKJV)

17 but of the tree of the knowledge of good and evil you shall not eat, for in the day that you eat of it you shall surely die."

Genesis 41:8 (NKJV)

8 Now it came to pass in the morning that his spirit was troubled, and he sent and called for all the magicians of Egypt and all its wise men. And Pharaoh told them his dreams, but *there was* no one who could interpret them for Pharaoh.

Exodus 31:3 (NKJV)

3 And I have filled him with the Spirit of God, in wisdom, in understanding, in knowledge, and in all *manner of* workmanship,

Exodus 35:31 (NKJV)

31 and He has filled him with the Spirit of God, in wisdom and understanding, in knowledge and all manner of workmanship,

Numbers 21:23 (NKJV)

23 But Sihon would not allow Israel to pass through his territory. So Sihon gathered all his people together and went out against Israel in the wilderness, and he came to Jahaz and fought against Israel.

Numbers 24:2 (NKJV)

2 And Balaam raised his eyes, and saw Israel encamped according to their tribes; and the Spirit of God came upon him.

Numbers 27:18 (NKJV)

18 And the LORD said to Moses: "Take Joshua the son of Nun with you, a man in whom *is* the Spirit, and lay your hand on him;

Deuteronomy 2:26-31 (NKJV)

[26] "And I sent messengers from the Wilderness of Kedemoth to Sihon king of Heshbon, with words of peace, saying,

[27] 'Let me pass through your land; I will keep strictly to the road, and I will turn neither to the right nor to the left.

[28] You shall sell me food for money, that I may eat, and give me water for money, that I may drink; only let me pass through on foot,

[29] just as the descendants of Esau who dwell in Seir and the Moabites who dwell in Ar did for me, until I cross the Jordan to the land which the LORD our God is giving us.'

[30] But Sihon king of Heshbon would not let us pass through, for the LORD your God hardened his spirit and made his heart obstinate, that He might deliver him into your hand, as *it is* this day.

[31] And the LORD said to me, 'See, I have begun to give Sihon and his land over to you. Begin to possess *it,* that you may inherit his land.'

Judges 3:10 (NKJV)

[10] The Spirit of the LORD came upon him, and he judged Israel. He went out to war, and the LORD delivered Cushan-Rishathaim king of Mesopotamia into his hand; and his hand prevailed over Cushan-Rishathaim.

Judges 6:34 (NKJV)

[34] But the Spirit of the LORD came upon Gideon; then he blew the trumpet, and the Abiezrites gathered behind him.

Judges 11:29 (NKJV)

[29] Then the Spirit of the LORD came upon Jephthah, and he passed through Gilead and Manasseh, and passed through Mizpah of Gilead; and from Mizpah of Gilead he advanced *toward* the people of Ammon.

Judges 13:25 (NKJV)

[25] And the Spirit of the LORD began to move upon him at Mahaneh Dan between Zorah and Eshtaol.

Judges 14:6 (NKJV)

[6] And the Spirit of the LORD came mightily upon him, and he tore the lion apart as one would have torn apart a young goat, though *he had* nothing in his hand. But he did not tell his father or his mother what he had done.

Judges 14:19 (NKJV)

[19] Then the Spirit of the LORD came upon him mightily, and he went down to Ashkelon and killed thirty of their men, took their apparel, and gave the changes *of clothing* to those who had explained the riddle. So his anger was aroused, and he went back up to his father's house.

Judges 15:14 (NKJV)

[14] When he came to Lehi, the Philistines came shouting against him. Then the Spirit of the LORD came mightily upon him; and the ropes that *were* on his arms became like flax that is burned with fire, and his bonds broke loose from his hands.

Judges 15:19 (NKJV)

[19] So God split the hollow place that *is* in Lehi, and water came out, and he drank; and his spirit returned, and he revived. Therefore he called its name En Hakkore, which is in Lehi to this day.

1 Samuel 10:6 (NKJV)

[6] Then the Spirit of the LORD will come upon you, and you will prophesy with them and be turned into another man.

1 Samuel 10:10 (NKJV)

[10] When they came there to the hill, there was a group of prophets to meet him; then the Spirit of God came upon him, and he prophesied among them.

1 Samuel 11:6 (NKJV)

[6] Then the Spirit of God came upon Saul when he heard this news, and his anger was greatly aroused.

1 Samuel 15:11 (NKJV)

[11] "I greatly regret that I have set up Saul *as* king, for he has turned back from following Me, and has not performed My commandments." And it grieved Samuel, and he cried out to the LORD all night.

1 Samuel 16:13 (NKJV)

[13] Then Samuel took the horn of oil and anointed him in the midst of his brothers; and the Spirit of the LORD came upon David from that day forward. So Samuel arose and went to Ramah.

1 Samuel 16:14 (NKJV)

[14] But the Spirit of the LORD departed from Saul, and a distressing spirit from the LORD troubled him.

1 Samuel 16:23 (NKJV)

[23] And so it was, whenever the spirit from God was upon Saul, that David would take a harp and play *it* with his hand. Then Saul would become refreshed and well, and the distressing spirit would depart from him.

1 Samuel 18:1-16 (NKJV)

[1] Now when he had finished speaking to Saul, the soul of Jonathan was knit to the soul of David, and Jonathan loved him as his own soul.

[2] Saul took him that day, and would not let him go home to his father's house anymore.

[3] Then Jonathan and David made a covenant, because he loved him as his own soul.

[4] And Jonathan took off the robe that *was* on him and gave it to David, with his armor, even to his sword and his bow and his belt.

5 So David went out wherever Saul sent him, *and* behaved wisely. And Saul set him over the men of war, and he was accepted in the sight of all the people and also in the sight of Saul's servants.

6 Now it had happened as they were coming *home,* when David was returning from the slaughter of the Philistine, that the women had come out of all the cities of Israel, singing and dancing, to meet King Saul, with tambourines, with joy, and with musical instruments.

7 So the women sang as they danced, and said: "Saul has slain his thousands, And David his ten thousands."

8 Then Saul was very angry, and the saying displeased him; and he said, "They have ascribed to David ten thousands, and to me they have ascribed *only* thousands. Now *what* more can he have but the kingdom?"

9 So Saul eyed David from that day forward.

10 And it happened on the next day that the distressing spirit from God came upon Saul, and he prophesied inside the house. So David played *music* with his hand, as at other times; but *there was* a spear in Saul's hand.

11 And Saul cast the spear, for he said, "I will pin David to the wall!" But David escaped his presence twice.

12 Now Saul was afraid of David, because the LORD was with him, but had departed from Saul.

13 Therefore Saul removed him from his presence, and made him his captain over a thousand; and he went out and came in before the people.

14 And David behaved wisely in all his ways, and the LORD *was* with him.

15 Therefore, when Saul saw that he behaved very wisely, he was afraid of him.

16 But all Israel and Judah loved David, because he went out and came in before them.

1 Samuel 19:1-10 (NKJV)

1 Now Saul spoke to Jonathan his son and to all his servants, that they should kill David; but Jonathan, Saul's son, delighted greatly in David.

2 So Jonathan told David, saying, "My father Saul seeks to kill you. Therefore please be on your guard until morning, and stay in a secret *place* and hide.

3 And I will go out and stand beside my father in the field where you *are,* and I will speak with my father about you. Then what I observe, I will tell you."

4 Thus Jonathan spoke well of David to Saul his father, and said to him, "Let not the king sin against his servant, against David, because he has not sinned against you, and because his works *have been* very good toward you.

5 For he took his life in his hands and killed the Philistine, and the LORD brought about a great deliverance for all Israel. You saw *it* and rejoiced. Why then will you sin against innocent blood, to kill David without a cause?"

6 So Saul heeded the voice of Jonathan, and Saul swore, "*As* the LORD lives, he shall not be killed."

7 Then Jonathan called David, and Jonathan told him all these things. So Jonathan brought David to Saul, and he was in his presence as in times past.

8 And there was war again; and David went out and fought with the Philistines, and struck them with a mighty blow, and they fled from him.

9 Now the distressing spirit from the LORD came upon Saul as he sat in his house with his spear in his hand. And David was playing *music* with *his* hand.

10 Then Saul sought to pin David to the wall with the spear, but he slipped away from Saul's presence; and he drove the spear into the wall. So David fled and escaped that night.

1 Kings 22:21 (NKJV)

21 Then a spirit came forward and stood before the LORD, and said, 'I will persuade him.'

2 Kings 2:16 (NKJV)

16 Then they said to him, "Look now, there are fifty strong men with your servants. Please let them go and search for your master, lest perhaps the Spirit of the LORD has taken him up and cast him upon some mountain or into some valley." And he said, "You shall not send anyone."

1 Chronicles 5:26 (NKJV)

26 So the God of Israel stirred up the spirit of Pul king of Assyria, that is, Tiglath-Pileser king of Assyria. He carried the Reubenites, the Gadites, and the half-tribe of Manasseh into captivity. He took them to Halah, Habor, Hara, and the river of Gozan to this day.

1 Chronicles 12:18 (NKJV)

18 Then the Spirit came upon Amasai, chief of the captains, *and he said:* "*We are* yours, O David; We *are* on your side, O son of Jesse! Peace, peace to you, And peace to your helpers! For your God helps you." So David received them, and made them captains of the troop.

2 Chronicles 9:4 (NKJV)

4 the food on his table, the seating of his servants, the service of his waiters and their apparel, his cupbearers and their apparel, and his entryway by which he went up to the house of the LORD, there was no more spirit in her.

2 Chronicles 15:1 (NKJV)

1 Now the Spirit of God came upon Azariah the son of Oded.

2 Chronicles 18:20-23 (NKJV)

20 Then a spirit came forward and stood before the LORD, and said, 'I will persuade him.' The LORD said to him, 'In what way?'

21 So he said, 'I will go out and be a lying spirit in the mouth of all his prophets.' And *the Lord* said, 'You shall persuade *him* and also prevail; go out and do so.'

[22] Therefore look! The LORD has put a lying spirit in the mouth of these prophets of yours, and the LORD has declared disaster against you."

[23] Then Zedekiah the son of Chenaanah went near and struck Micaiah on the cheek, and said, "Which way did the spirit from the LORD go from me to speak to you?"

2 Chronicles 20:14 (NKJV)

[14] Then the Spirit of the LORD came upon Jahaziel the son of Zechariah, the son of Benaiah, the son of Jeiel, the son of Mattaniah, a Levite of the sons of Asaph, in the midst of the assembly.

2 Chronicles 36:22 (NKJV)

[22] Now in the first year of Cyrus king of Persia, that the word of the LORD by the mouth of Jeremiah might be fulfilled, the LORD stirred up the spirit of Cyrus king of Persia, so that he made a proclamation throughout all his kingdom, and also *put it* in writing, saying,

Ezra 1:1 (NKJV)

[1] Now in the first year of Cyrus king of Persia, that the word of the LORD by the mouth of Jeremiah might be fulfilled, the LORD stirred up the spirit of Cyrus king of Persia, so that he made a proclamation throughout all his kingdom, and also *put it* in writing, saying,

Ezra 1:5 (NKJV)

[5] Then the heads of the fathers' *houses* of Judah and Benjamin, and the priests and the Levites, with all whose spirits God had moved, arose to go up and build the house of the LORD which *is* in Jerusalem.

Job 6:1-7 (NKJV)

[1] Then Job answered and said:

[2] "Oh, that my grief were fully weighed, And my calamity laid with it on the scales!

[3] For then it would be heavier than the sand of the sea– Therefore my words have been rash.

[4] For the arrows of the Almighty *are* within me; My spirit drinks in their poison; The terrors of God are arrayed against me.

[5] Does the wild donkey bray when it has grass, Or does the ox low over its fodder?

[6] Can flavorless food be eaten without salt? Or is there *any* taste in the white of an egg?

[7] My soul refuses to touch them; They *are* as loathsome food to me.

Job 21:4 (NKJV)

[4] "As for me, *is* my complaint against man? And if *it were,* why should I not be impatient?

Job 26:4 (NKJV)

[4] To whom have you uttered words? And whose spirit came from you?

Job 32:8 (NKJV)

[8] But *there is* a spirit in man, And the breath of the Almighty gives him understanding.

Job 32:16-22 (NKJV)

[16] And I have waited, because they did not speak, Because they stood still *and* answered no more.

[17] I also will answer my part, I too will declare my opinion.

[18] For I am full of words; The spirit within me compels me.

[19] Indeed my belly *is* like wine *that* has no vent; It is ready to burst like new wineskins.

[20] I will speak, that I may find relief; I must open my lips and answer.

[21] Let me not, I pray, show partiality to anyone; Nor let me flatter any man.

[22] For I do not know how to flatter, *Else* my Maker would soon take me away.

Psalm 22:28 (NKJV)

[28] For the kingdom *is* the LORD'S, And He rules over the nations.

Psalm 77:3 (NKJV)

[3] I remembered God, and was troubled; I complained, and my spirit was overwhelmed. Selah

Psalm 115:3 (NKJV)

[3] But our God *is* in heaven; He does whatever He pleases.

Psalm 142:3 (NKJV)

[3] When my spirit was overwhelmed within me, Then You knew my path. In the way in which I walk They have secretly set a snare for me.

Psalm 143:4 (NKJV)

[4] Therefore my spirit is overwhelmed within me; My heart within me is distressed.

Proverbs 14:10 (NKJV)

[10] The heart knows its own bitterness, And a stranger does not share its joy.

Proverbs 15:4 (NKJV)

[4] A wholesome tongue *is* a tree of life, But perverseness in it breaks the spirit.

Proverbs 15:30 (NKJV)

[30] The light of the eyes rejoices the heart, *And* a good report makes the bones healthy.

Ezekiel 3:14 (NKJV)

14 So the Spirit lifted me up and took me away, and I went in bitterness, in the heat of my spirit; but the hand of the LORD was strong upon me.

Ezekiel 27:31 (NKJV)

31 They will shave themselves completely bald because of you, Gird themselves with sackcloth, And weep for you With bitterness of heart *and* bitter wailing.

Daniel 2:1 (NKJV)

1 Now in the second year of Nebuchadnezzar's reign, Nebuchadnezzar had dreams; and his spirit was *so* troubled that his sleep left him.

Daniel 2:2-4 (NKJV)

2 Then the king gave the command to call the magicians, the astrologers, the sorcerers, and the Chaldeans to tell the king his dreams. So they came and stood before the king.

3 And the king said to them, "I have had a dream, and my spirit is anxious to know the dream."

4 Then the Chaldeans spoke to the king in Aramaic, "O king, live forever! Tell your servants the dream, and we will give the interpretation."

Daniel 4:35 (NKJV)

35 All the inhabitants of the earth *are* reputed as nothing; He does according to His will in the army of heaven And *among* the inhabitants of the earth. No one can restrain His hand Or say to Him, "What have You done?"

Mark 7:21-23 (NKJV)

21 For from within, out of the heart of men, proceed evil thoughts, adulteries, fornications, murders,

22 thefts, covetousness, wickedness, deceit, lewdness, an evil eye, blasphemy, pride, foolishness.

23 All these evil things come from within and defile a man."

Romans 5:12-21 (NKJV)

12 Therefore, just as through one man sin entered the world, and death through sin, and thus death spread to all men, because all sinned–

13 (For until the law sin was in the world, but sin is not imputed when there is no law.

14 Nevertheless death reigned from Adam to Moses, even over those who had not sinned according to the likeness of the transgression of Adam, who is a type of Him who was to come.

15 But the free gift *is* not like the offense. For if by the one man's offense many died, much more the grace of God and the gift by the grace of the one Man, Jesus Christ, abounded to many.

16 And the gift *is* not like *that which came* through the one who sinned. For the judgment *which came* from one *offense resulted* in condemnation, but the free gift *which came* from many offenses *resulted* in justification.

17 For if by the one man's offense death reigned through the one, much more those who receive abundance of grace and of the gift of righteousness will reign in life through the One, Jesus Christ.)

18 Therefore, as through one man's offense *judgment* came to all men, resulting in condemnation, even so through one Man's righteous act *the free gift came* to all men, resulting in justification of life.

19 For as by one man's disobedience many were made sinners, so also by one Man's obedience many will be made righteous.

20 Moreover the law entered that the offense might abound. But where sin abounded, grace abounded much more,

[21] so that as sin reigned in death, even so grace might reign through righteousness to eternal life through Jesus Christ our Lord.

1 Timothy 6:15 (NKJV)

[15] which He will manifest in His own time, *He who is* the blessed and only Potentate, the King of kings and Lord of lords,

Chapter Five – How to Characterize an emotion

Tooby and Cosmides (2008) suggested there was a way to characterize an emotion. One must identify the following properties of environments and mechanisms. 1) An evolutionarily recurrent situation or condition; 2) The adaptive problem i.e. identify which organismic states and behavioral sequences will lead to the best average functional outcome for the remainder of the lifespan, given the situation or condition; 3) Cues that signal the presence of the situation; 4) Situation-detecting algorithms; 5) Algorithms that assign priorities; 6) An internal communication system; and 7) Each program and physiological mechanism must have associated algorithms that regulate how it responds to each emotional signal.

An Algorithm is defined as a procedure for solving a mathematical problem in a finite number or steps that frequently involves repetition of an operation. The step by step procedures include environmental and mechanical properties. In order to detect these properties a complex composite in the environment of evolutionary adaptedness is needed.

In this chapter, I suggest the way to characterize an emotion is based on the light of the spirit in the spirit of life in each human being. Whereby, the intensity of the light is equal to the emotion characterized. The environment adaptation is only relative to the light manifested within the spirit of life. The spirit within the spirit of life is causal of human emotion and not the environment or mechanistic properties.

Tooby and Cosmides theorize an emotion lies dormant waiting for some condition to occur. Therefore, the mechanism of condition is cued. If the cue is equal to a functional outcome as seen in a behavioral sequence, then environmental stimuli has circular process directed toward the cue. This hypothesis has no theological foundation.

In order to characterize an emotion, I believe it is significant to understand what is being characterized from the core of the heart. Namely what does the scriptures say about the core?

Within the core of the heart, the life essence is a multiplicity of properties. The spirit illumines the inner spirit with light whereby producing any of the following. Each characterization of human emotion can be relative of past, present, or future emotional experience. Therefore, he may perceive (Deuteronomy 29:4), cheer (Ecclesiastes 11:9), have inclination (Numbers 15:39) i.e. can be hardened (Exodus 4:21), have integrity (Genesis 20:5), faint (Genesis 45:26), be willing (Exodus 35:5), have wisdom (Exodus 35:5), have sorrow (Leviticus 26:16), be astonished (Deuteronomy 28:28), have joyfulness and gladness (Deuteronomy 28:47), tremble (Deuteronomy 28:65), imagine (Deuteronomy 29:19), think (Judges 5:15-16), be grieved (1 Samuel 2:33), be naughty (1 Samuel 17:28), desire (1 Samuel 28:5), have uprightness (1 Kings 3:6), understand (1 Kings 3:9), lie (1 Kings 22:23), sing (Job 29:13), be glad (Psalm 16:9), rejoice (Psalm 19:8), meditate (Psalm 19:14), pant (Psalm 38:10), be hot (Psalm 39:3), gather iniquity (Psalm 41:6), be broken and contrite (Psalm 51:17), overwhelmed (Psalm 61:2), broken (Psalm 69:20), forward (Psalm 101:4) i.e. habitually disposed to disobedience and opposition, strengthened (Psalm 104:15), wounded (Psalm 109:22), imagine (Psalm 140:2), know (Proverbs 14:10), fret (Proverbs 19:3) i.e. to cause to suffer emotional strain, study (Proverbs 24:2), show pride and stoutness (Isaiah 9:9), be fearful (Isaiah 35:4), be deceived (Isaiah 44:20), revolting and rebellious (Jeremiah 5:23), walk (Ezekiel 11:21), have bitterness (Ezekiel 27:31), have unbelief and hardness (Mark 16:14), ponder (Luke 2:19), slow (Luke 24:25), and have intent (Hebrews 4:12).

According to the Scriptures, the heart makes you emotional. It is the source by which human beings experience emotion. The physiological brain does not have etiological causality. The life of the spirit of life is lived out in the soul and human body. As every characterization of the spirit as specified above persuades man, God's sovereignty determines prevailing completion (1 Kings 22:22).

Human emotion does not adapt to its environment or have substructures whereby the human brain organizes the aspectual differences of emotion. In fact, the spirit within every human being causes every characterization of emotion in man. Each human being can only walk in the "ways of the heart" (Ecclesiastes 11:9, 2:10). Just as there are many 'ways of the heart' so man is limited by those ways.

To characterize an emotion is to distinguish each emotion as separate. By placing each emotion on a ten point scale where zero is the lowest and ten is the greatest would validate difference and degree. This would distinguish difference. However, it would not delineate every difference.

Another way to characterize emotion is through maturation. Throughout the lifespan of a human being, individual spirits develop usage of difference in emotion. The difference may be discrete periods of transition where continuity is a gradual process. The continuity is regulated by the spirit of life. It would not be regulated by chronological age or biological/physiological development.

From prenatal development throughout the life of the human being, emotional expression is limited by the spirit. Although limited in usage, a human integrated body, soul, and spirit has limitation. Therefore, it would be generalized to others who vary in age, race, ethnic background, education, religion, and gender. Moreover, it is not the person with environmental limitations but their spirit which inhibits.

Lewis (2008) stated in order for an emotion to occur, some stimulus event must trigger a change in the state of the organism. The state of the organism can be a change in an idea, or in the physiological state of the organism. He posited the triggering event may either be external or internal stimulus. External stimulus may be a loud noise or a separation from a loved one. An internal elicitor may range from changes in specific physiological states to complex cognitive activities.

To further explain how the heart makes a human being emotional I have confronted psychological empirical studies which posit environmental properties whereby neuronal constructs are etiological. However, these studies are void of theological truth. We now know the core of the heart of man regulates the emotional impelling movement so that a human may experience emotion.

However, there is one more level downward which supports theological etiology. First, according to Proverbs 15, the heart is causality for emotion. I have already given several biblical texts to support and validate this phenomenon. Second, it is the eye of the spirit which "sees" and thereby within .05 seconds human behavior is manifested. On April 06, 2009 the Spirit said to me, "There is a delay of five seconds in the spirits movement and the behavior of a human being." Third, the light (Hebrew *'ma or'*, which means luminous, from the Hebrew word *'or'*, meaning to be [causative make] luminous) of the eye rejoices the heart.

Consider this analogy of a train with cars on a train track. The fuel for the engine of the train is the light for the eye. The engine of the train is the eye of the heart. The engine is the core of the heart. The light (luminous) is the primary source. Scripture states God caused the light to be set up (Psalm 74:16). Just as God made two lights, one greater and one lesser (Genesis 1:16), so the light of the eyes is the very essence of the light of God (Hebrews 1:1-3, John 8:12).

Do not misunderstand this does not make you God. Human beings are born into sin. Sin is affective within our entire being. Every part of man is fully effected by the law of sin (Romans 5:12-18). When a human being confesses Jesus as Lord (Romans 10:9) from their heart, he is converted, forgiven of sin, and adopted into God's family. At this moment, our spirits permeate the light of God (Colossians 1:12; 1 Thessalonians 5:5; 2 Peter 1:19; 1 John 1:5, 7).

KEY WORDS

1. Core of the heart
2. Emotional expression
3. Intensity
4. Light of the spirit
5. Ways of the heart

KEY QUESTIONS

1. How is the intensity of light of a spirit characterized as emotion?
2. What takes place in the core of the heart?
3. What makes a human being emotional?
4. How does maturation characterized emotion?
5. Explain how the spirit in the core of the heart impels emotional movement?

Quick Scripture Reference Guide

Genesis 1:16 (NKJV)

16 Then God made two great lights: the greater light to rule the day, and the lesser light to rule the night. *He made* the stars also.

Genesis 20:5 (NKJV)

5 Did he not say to me, 'She *is* my sister'? And she, even she herself said, 'He *is* my brother.' In the integrity of my heart and innocence of my hands I have done this."

Genesis 45:26 (NKJV)

26 And they told him, saying, "Joseph *is* still alive, and he *is* governor over all the land of Egypt." And Jacob's heart stood still, because he did not believe them.

Exodus 4:21 (NKJV)

21 And the LORD said to Moses, "When you go back to Egypt, see that you do all those wonders before Pharaoh which I have put in your hand. But I will harden his heart, so that he will not let the people go.

Exodus 35:5-6 (NKJV)

5 'Take from among you an offering to the LORD. Whoever *is* of a willing heart, let him bring it as an offering to the LORD: gold, silver, and bronze;

6 blue, purple, and scarlet *thread,* fine linen, and goats' *hair;*

Leviticus 26:16 (NKJV)

16 I also will do this to you: I will even appoint terror over you, wasting disease and fever which shall consume the eyes and cause sorrow of heart. And you shall sow your seed in vain, for your enemies shall eat it.

Numbers 15:39 (NKJV)

[39] And you shall have the tassel, that you may look upon it and remember all the commandments of the LORD and do them, and that you *may* not follow the harlotry to which your own heart and your own eyes are inclined,

Deuteronomy 28:28 (NKJV)

[28] The LORD will strike you with madness and blindness and confusion of heart.

Deuteronomy 28:47 (NKJV)

[47] "Because you did not serve the LORD your God with joy and gladness of heart, for the abundance of everything,

Deuteronomy 28:65 (NKJV)

[65] And among those nations you shall find no rest, nor shall the sole of your foot have a resting place; but there the LORD will give you a trembling heart, failing eyes, and anguish of soul.

Deuteronomy 29:4 (NKJV)

[4] Yet the LORD has not given you a heart to perceive and eyes to see and ears to hear, to this *very* day.

Deuteronomy 29:19 (NKJV)

[19] and so it may not happen, when he hears the words of this curse, that he blesses himself in his heart, saying, 'I shall have peace, even though I follow the dictates of my heart'–as though the drunkard could be included with the sober.

Judges 5:15-16 (NKJV)

[15] And the princes of Issachar *were* with Deborah; As Issachar, so *was* Barak Sent into the valley under his command; Among the divisions of Reuben *There were* great resolves of heart.

[16] Why did you sit among the sheepfolds, To hear the pipings for the flocks? The divisions of Reuben have great searchings of heart.

1 Samuel 2:33 (NKJV)

[33] But any of your men *whom* I do not cut off from My altar shall consume your eyes and grieve your heart. And all the descendants of your house shall die in the flower of their age.

1 Samuel 17:28 (NKJV)

[28] Now Eliab his oldest brother heard when he spoke to the men; and Eliab's anger was aroused against David, and he said, "Why did you come down here? And with whom have you left those few sheep in the wilderness? I know your pride and the insolence of your heart, for you have c **1**

1 Samuel 28:5 (NKJV)

[5] When Saul saw the army of the Philistines, he was afraid, and his heart trembled greatly.

1 Kings 3:6 (NKJV)

[6] And Solomon said: "You have shown great mercy to Your servant David my father, because he walked before You in truth, in righteousness, and in uprightness of heart with You; You have continued this great kindness for him, and You have given him a son to sit on his throne, as *it is* this day.

1 Kings 3:9 (NKJV)

[9] Therefore give to Your servant an understanding heart to judge Your people, that I may discern between good and evil. For who is able to judge this great people of Yours?"

1 Kings 22:22 (NKJV)

[22] The LORD said to him, 'In what way?' So he said, 'I will go out and be a lying spirit in the mouth of all his prophets.' And the LORD said, 'You shall persuade *him,* and also prevail. Go out and do so.'

1 Kings 22:23 (NKJV)

[23] Therefore look! The LORD has put a lying spirit in the mouth of all these prophets of yours, and the LORD has declared disaster against you."

Job 29:13 (NKJV)

[13] The blessing of a perishing *man* came upon me, And I caused the widow's heart to sing for joy.

Psalm 16:9 (NKJV)

[9] Therefore my heart is glad, and my glory rejoices; My flesh also will rest in hope.

Psalm 19:8 (NKJV)

[8] The statutes of the LORD *are* right, rejoicing the heart; The commandment of the LORD *is* pure, enlightening the eyes;

Psalm 19:14 (NKJV)

[14] Let the words of my mouth and the meditation of my heart Be acceptable in Your sight, O LORD, my strength and my Redeemer.

Psalm 38:10 (NKJV)

[10] My heart pants, my strength fails me; As for the light of my eyes, it also has gone from me.

Psalm 39:3 (NKJV)

[3] My heart was hot within me; While I was musing, the fire burned. *Then* I spoke with my tongue:

Psalm 41:6 (NKJV)

[6] And if he comes to see *me,* he speaks lies; His heart gathers iniquity to itself; *When* he goes out, he tells *it.*

Psalm 51:17 (NKJV)

[17] The sacrifices of God *are* a broken spirit, A broken and a contrite heart– These, O God, You will not despise.

Psalm 61:2 (NKJV)

[2] From the end of the earth I will cry to You, When my heart is overwhelmed; Lead me to the rock that is higher than I.

Psalm 69:20 (NKJV)

[20] Reproach has broken my heart, And I am full of heaviness; I looked *for someone* to take pity, but *there was* none; And for comforters, but I found none.

Psalm 74:16 (NKJV)

[16] The day *is* Yours, the night also *is* Yours; You have prepared the light and the sun.

Psalm 101:4 (NKJV)

[4] A perverse heart shall depart from me; I will not know wickedness.

Psalm 104:15 (NKJV)

[15] And wine *that* makes glad the heart of man, Oil to make *his* face shine, And bread *which* strengthens man's heart.

Psalm 109:22 (NKJV)

[22] For I *am* poor and needy, And my heart is wounded within me.

Psalm 140:2 (NKJV)

[2] Who plan evil things in *their* hearts; They continually gather together *for* war.

Proverbs 14:10 (NKJV)

[10] The heart knows its own bitterness, And a stranger does not share its joy.

Proverbs 19:3 (NKJV)

[3] The foolishness of a man twists his way, And his heart frets against the LORD.

Proverbs 24:2 (NKJV)

[2] For their heart devises violence, And their lips talk of troublemaking.

Ecclesiastes 2:10 (NKJV)

[10] Whatever my eyes desired I did not keep from them. I did not withhold my heart from any pleasure, For my heart rejoiced in all my labor; And this was my reward from all my labor.

Ecclesiastes 11:9 (NKJV)

[9] Rejoice, O young man, in your youth, And let your heart cheer you in the days of your youth; Walk in the ways of your heart, And in the sight of your eyes; But know that for all these God will bring you into judgment.

Isaiah 9:9 (NKJV)

[9] All the people will know– Ephraim and the inhabitant of Samaria– Who say in pride and arrogance of heart:

Isaiah 35:4 (NKJV)

[4] Say to those *who are* fearful-hearted, "Be strong, do not fear! Behold, your God will come *with* vengeance, *With* the recompense of God; He will come and save you."

Isaiah 44:20 (NKJV)

[20] He feeds on ashes; A deceived heart has turned him aside; And he cannot deliver his soul, Nor say, "*Is there* not a lie in my right hand?"

Jeremiah 5:23 (NKJV)

[23] But this people has a defiant and rebellious heart; They have revolted and departed.

Ezekiel 11:21 (NKJV)

[21] But *as for those* whose hearts follow the desire for their detestable things and their abominations, I will recompense their deeds on their own heads," says the Lord GOD.

Ezekiel 27:31 (NKJV)

[31] They will shave themselves completely bald because of you, Gird themselves with sackcloth, And weep for you With bitterness of heart *and* bitter wailing.

Mark 16:14 (NKJV)

[14] Later He appeared to the eleven as they sat at the table; and He rebuked their unbelief and hardness of heart, because they did not believe those who had seen Him after He had risen.

Luke 2:19 (NKJV)

[19] But Mary kept all these things and pondered *them* in her heart.

Luke 24:25 (NKJV)

[25] Then He said to them, "O foolish ones, and slow of heart to believe in all that the prophets have spoken!

John 8:12 (NKJV)

[12] Then Jesus spoke to them again, saying, "I am the light of the world. He who follows Me shall not walk in darkness, but have the light of life."

Romans 5:12-18 (NKJV)

[12] Therefore, just as through one man sin entered the world, and death through sin, and thus death spread to all men, because all sinned–

[13] (For until the law sin was in the world, but sin is not imputed when there is no law.

[14] Nevertheless death reigned from Adam to Moses, even over those who had not sinned according to the likeness of the transgression of Adam, who is a type of Him who was to come.

[15] But the free gift *is* not like the offense. For if by the one man's offense many died, much more the grace of God and the gift by the grace of the one Man, Jesus Christ, abounded to many.

[16] And the gift *is* not like *that which came* through the one who sinned. For the judgment *which came* from one *offense resulted* in condemnation, but the free gift *which came* from many offenses *resulted* in justification.

[17] For if by the one man's offense death reigned through the one, much more those who receive abundance of grace and of the gift of righteousness will reign in life through the One, Jesus Christ.)

[18] Therefore, as through one man's offense *judgment* came to all men, resulting in condemnation, even so through one Man's righteous act *the free gift came* to all men, resulting in justification of life.

Romans 10:9 (NKJV)

[9] that if you confess with your mouth the Lord Jesus and believe in your heart that God has raised Him from the dead, you will be saved.

Colossians 1:12 (NKJV)

[12] giving thanks to the Father who has qualified us to be partakers of the inheritance of the saints in the light.

1 Thessalonians 5:5 (NKJV)

[5] You are all sons of light and sons of the day. We are not of the night nor of darkness.

Hebrews 1:1-3 (NKJV)

[1] God, who at various times and in various ways spoke in time past to the fathers by the prophets,

[2] has in these last days spoken to us by *His* Son, whom He has appointed heir of all things, through whom also He made the worlds;

[3] who being the brightness of *His* glory and the express image of His person, and upholding all things by the word of His power, when He had by Himself purged our sins, sat down at the right hand of the Majesty on high,

Hebrews 4:11-12 (NKJV)

[11] Let us therefore be diligent to enter that rest, lest anyone fall according to the same example of disobedience.

[12] For the word of God *is* living and powerful, and sharper than any two-edged sword, piercing even to the division of soul and spirit, and of joints and marrow, and is a discerner of the thoughts and intents of the heart.

2 Peter 1:19 (NKJV)

[19] And so we have the prophetic word confirmed, which you do well to heed as a light that shines in a dark place, until the day dawns and the morning star rises in your hearts;

1 John 1:5-7 (NKJV)

[5] This is the message which we have heard from Him and declare to you, that God is light and in Him is no darkness at all.

[6] If we say that we have fellowship with Him, and walk in darkness, we lie and do not practice the truth.

[7] But if we walk in the light as He is in the light, we have fellowship with one another, and the blood of Jesus Christ His Son cleanses us from all sin.

Chapter Six – The Emotional Affect of Spirit

You might agree with me that at the moment of conception, the full and complete body, soul, and spirit are in union. Through dimension life is active and light (the life of the spirit) expands within the soul to adult physical stature. The soul contains the light and light fully encompasses the soul. No dimensional space within soul is void of light. The physical substance of a human being has full affect from the spirit.

According to Scripture the physiological substance of man is to rule over the spiritual life (Proverbs 25:28). Even though the spiritual essence is human cognition, cognitive operations, and cognitive structures, the spirit remains the lamp of life (Proverbs 20:27, Isaiah 38:16). In this chapter the research will show where emotion comes from and how that emotion affects behavior.

There is a phenomenon with significant implications which I will attempt to explain. The phenomenon is reciprocity of spirits. The ability of a spirit to interact with the human spirit is one issue. Another is the ability of a spirit to dwell inside the human spirit whereby behavioral modifications are made. Yet still, do the Scriptures support such a dynamic? The answer is yes it does.

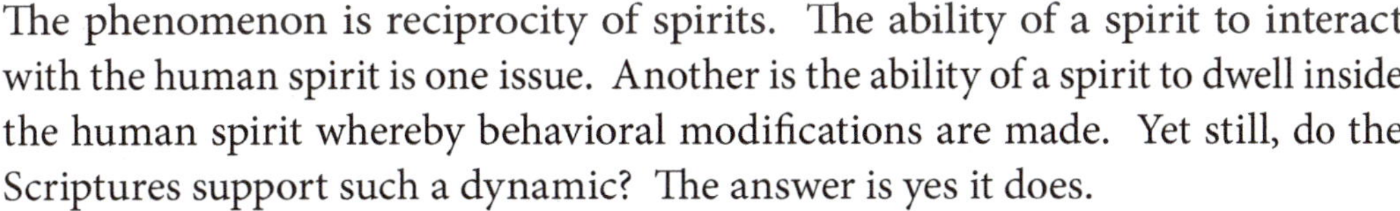

In Numbers 11, Moses went out and told the people the words of the Lord, and he gathered the seventy men of the elders of the people and placed them around the tabernacle. Then the Lord came down in the cloud, and spoke to him, and *took of the spirit that was upon him*, and placed the same upon the seventy elders. And it happened, when the Spirit rested upon them, that they prophesied...But two men had remained in the camp, Eldad, and Medad. And the spirit rested upon them...Joshua said, "Moses my lord, forbid them!" Then Moses said to him, "Are you zealous for my sake? Oh, that all the Lord's people were prophets and the Lord would put His spirit upon them!"

When the Lord took of the spirit which was upon Moses, there was no apparent change in Moses. In other words, neither his character nor his personality revealed any change. To remove any essence of the spirit from Moses did not change Moses. The men who received this spirit were changed in that they began to prophecy. No other behavioral changes were noticed within the camp. The experience of placing another spirit upon each of the seventy elders revealed strong affect. Immediately when the spirit rested upon the seventy, they began to prophecy.

When another spirit rests upon a human being within the spirit of life, the spirit remains until the manifestation is completed. There was no behavioral control, an inability to stop the action, and notice the strength of spirit. The physiological/ biological substance of man was incapable of controlling the spirit.

No one (Hebrew *echad*, meaning united i.e. one) has power (Hebrew *shalliyt*, meaning potent [a prince or warrior], (Hebrew *shalat*, meaning to dominate) over the spirit (Hebrew *ruwach*, meaning wind, breath i.e. a sensible exhalation, to blow) to retain (Hebrew *kala*, meaning to restrict, by act or word) the spirit [same meaning as before] (Ecclesiastes 8:8). Therefore, no human being has the dominating power to restrict the spirit. The spirit has full movement and mobility while in the spirit of life of the human being. Moreover, the movement is restricted to the spirit.

In Numbers 14:24, 32:12; and Joshua 14:6-8 Caleb was given one additional spirit. The other men who were with him sent by Moses to spy out the land, did not have this spirit. Caleb had another spirit with him and he followed God fully. The ten men saw the same land, people, dwellings, and animals as Caleb and Joshua. Moreover, the ten men looked at the strength of the people, the size and walled cities and the size of the children of Anak. They said to Moses, "we are not able to go up against the people, for they are stronger than we are."

Caleb said "Let us go up at once and possess it; for we are well able to overcome it." Caleb was not afraid of the people, their size, or the children of Anak - "giants". Caleb reminded the people that the land was exceedingly good and if the Lord delights in us, then he will bring them into this land and give it to them. He admonished them to not rebel against the Lord, and not be afraid of the people.

To rebel against the Lord was to not believe him. Caleb's spirit (Hebrew *ruwach*, meaning wind, breath) was different. The Spirit was (KJV) another (Hebrew *acher*, meaning hinder, be behind), and has followed (Hebrew *archar*, meaning the hind part, after) Me fully (Hebrew *male*, meaning full or filling).

Caleb's spirit followed God. The spirit that was given to Caleb followed the spirit of God. What the spirit in Caleb saw from earth, was the spirit of God in heaven. The spirit followed God fully. It did not take its eye off God. The indication of a multiplicity of dimension is revealed. While Caleb lived on earth in height, width, and depth, his spirit was able to see into heaven, which is dimension six. Where ever God went in heaven, the spirit in Caleb followed by "seeing".

Caleb did not show any psychological or behavioral dysfunction to his eleven friends. While looking throughout the land nothing was mentioned in Scripture to suggest Caleb had hallucinations or Schizotypal Personality Disorder (i.e. a pervasive pattern of social and interpersonal deficits marked by acute discomfort with and reduced capacity for, close relationships as well as by cognitive or perceptual distortions and eccentricities of behavior, beginning by early adulthood, and present in a variety of contexts, DSM-IV), behavior.

In Joshua 14:6-8, Caleb said, "I wholly (Hebrew mala, be full of) followed (Hebrew *archar*) the Lord my God". Caleb described the whole following began in his spirit and affected his conscious thought and behavior. When the spies returned and told Moses what had seen, Caleb and Joshua spoke up and tore their clothes in opposition to the ten other spies.

In Numbers 5:11-31 (NLT) Moses was told a person may receive a spirit without any knowledge. The behavior of that person will be affected by that spirit. The spirit has effectual ability. "Suppose a man's wife goes astray, and she is unfaithful to her husband and has sex with another man, but neither her husband nor anyone else knows about it. She has defiled herself, even though there was no witness and she was not caught in the act…or if a man becomes jealous and is suspicious that his wife has been unfaithful, the husband must present his wife before the Lord, and the priest will apply this entire ritual law to her."

If the spirit (Hebrew *ruwach*) of jealousy (Hebrew *qinah*, meaning envy) comes (Hebrew *abar*, meaning to cross over) i.e. to passover through the gateway (dimension four) [and come (i.e. to come is to see in your eye. What you see is reality. For the spirit to see, is reality through and beyond any dimension.) into his spirit of life in dimension 1, 2, and 3] upon him, he will be jealous (Hebrew *qana*, meaning to be [cause. make] zealous, i.e. jealous). For his wife to "go astray" or turn aside (KJV, Hebrew *satag*, meaning to deviate from duty) has behaved in sinful act. Her act was a choice without receiving a spirit to cause her to sin against her husband. His response to her was caused by the spirit of jealously.

He did not respond to his wife in zealous behavior. It was the spirit of jealousy in him that prompted and caused him to be jealous i.e. zealous is eagerness and ardent interest in pursuit of something. This new spirit was in addition to the spirit of life he had at conception.

According to Numbers 14:29-30, the spirit of jealousy may come without cause (i.e. spouse behavior). In fact, it is not subject to the willful sinful behavior of a spouse. Notice how close spirits watch our lives, behaviors, and activities. Unknown to our own activity, spirits are watching each of us from another dimension. In this case, they watched the woman turn aside from her husband and have sexual relations with another man. They watched her reactions to her husband. They watched her husband's behavior to his wife. Only one spirit was needed to cause the husband to be jealous of his wife. The affect of spirit is greater than human control.

Stearns (2008) posited jealousy has a female emotion and a contradiction of proper selflessness in love. Stets and Turner quoted Stryker (2008) which reported on the negative emotion of jealousy, said "when an identity is not being confirmed in a situation, an alternative identity that is being confirmed and that produces positive emotions such as satisfaction and happiness may move up the identity hierarchy and guide behavior."

Frijda (2008) described jealousy as a pain caused by rivalry, not just pain, nor anger, nor just despair; it is an interpersonal pain that can change its face at any moment. Tooby and Cosmides (2008) suggested jealousy is one of an aesthetic landscape of preferences. Jealousy like love or disgust is computational. It has an affectless, flavorless connotation which can be best understood as information-processing relations, that is, programs – with naturally selected functions which give operation to a patterned structure, as well as a set of neural circuits to implement it physically.

Fischer and Manstead (2008) theorized anger, jealousy, and contempt can clearly be socially dysfunctional. Rather than changing others' behaviors, they may irreparably damage the relationship between individuals or between groups, without achieving anything in terms of social control or social standing...social dysfunctionality is especially likely to occur if the social impact of one's emotions is not taken into account or if inappropriate appraisals of the social context are made.

The spirit of Jealousy makes and causes human beings to behave in a manner consistent with the spirits essence. Whether social dysfunctionality, divorce between a husband and his wife or death, the affect is caused by the spirit of Jealousy. Some spirits are called evil, while others are called good, familiar, right, etc. What a spirit is called does not infer the substance of essence.

In Judges 9:22-25 (NASB) "Now Abimelech ruled over Israel three years. Then God sent an evil spirit between Abimelech and the men of Shechem; and the men of Shechem dealt treacherously with Abimelech, so that the violence done to the seventy sons of Jerubbaal might come, and their blood might be laid on Abimelech their brother, who killed them, and on the men of Shechem, who strengthened his hands to kill his brothers. The men of Shechem set men in ambush against him on the tops of the mountains, and they robbed all who might pass by them along the road; and it was told to Abimelech."

God sent (Hebrew *Shalah*, meaning to send out, for, or away) an evil (Hebrew *rah*, meaning bad or evil from Hebrew *raa*, meaning properly to *spoil* (literal by *breaking* to pieces); figurative to *make* (or *be*) *good for nothing*, i.e. *bad* (physically, socially or morally) spirit (Hebrew *ruah*, meaning to breathe or wind). We are not told where the spirit was before God sent the evil spirit or the name of the evil spirit. We are told that God has power over the kingdom of evil spirits and uses their evil in the affairs of human beings.

The evil spirit moved the men of Shechem to rebel against Abimelech. One spirit in each of the men was moved with emotional significance. One spirit is able to move within many. The citizens of Shechem were directly affected by one spirit. Smith and Mackie (2008) suggested the affect of intergroup will elicit emotional responses, because the group becomes in a real sense an aspect of the person's psychological self. Simply put, under these conditions depersonalization causes the person to react to the world as a group member rather than a unique individual.

One spirit moved men to commit murder, be violent, express anger, rage, resentment, and experience frustration. This spirit "aided" or strengthened the men to effect their cognitive, perceptual, and motor processes. These negative emotions were not triggered by cultural differences or some level of anxiety from past events. Smith and Mackie posited emotional reactions can occur and motivate people to take specific sorts of action. Intergroup emotions should lead to actions specifically related to the intergroup situation.

Their hypothesis is centered on three ideas. First, that emotions such as anger, fear, disgust, or envy targeted specifically at an out-group *may relate* to perceptions, prejudiced attitudes, or discriminatory behaviors directed at the out-group. Second, people may experience emotions, positive or negative in-group directed emotions (such as group-based pride or collective guilt) and general affective feelings (such as happiness, anxiety, or irritation) that are based on group membership (Smith, et al.). Third, group identification makes the in-group part of the psychological self and hence makes group-relevant events or objects able to trigger emotions.

Could the men of Shechem murdered and rebelled against Abimelech without God sending an evil spirit? Do human beings have the emotional motivation minus the spirit to experience high levels of emotion? According to Scripture, all emotion comes from the spirit. The human brain does not have origination of emotion centered within its neuronal subsystems.

Pink (1930) defined the human will as the faculty of choice, the immediate cause of all action. To will is to choose and to choose is to decide between two or more alternatives. Willard (1998) explained will is the executive center of the self. Thus the center point of the spiritual in humans as well as in God is self-determination, also called freedom and creativity. Thiesson (1989) stated will is to choose between motives and to direct its subsequent activity according to the motive thus chosen.

According to Daniel 11:3; 8:4 "and do according to his will" (Hebrew *ratsown*, meaning delight from Hebrew *ratsah*, meaning to be pleased with; specifically to satisfy). Jesus explained the will of man in Matthew 16:24-25. The will (Greek *thelema*, meaning a determination taken from the Greek *Thelo*, meaning to determine) is human determination. I disagree with Willard that self-determination is the executive center of self. I posit self determination must include the physiological substance i.e. the human brain. Human determination without physiological substance to choose presupposes spirit determination.

Jesus explained origination of behavior of each human being proceeds out of the heart of man. It is in combination of spirit, soul, and body that self determination of choice has significance. For the men of Shechem to commit murder their delight proceeded (Greek *ekporeuomai*, meaning to depart, be discharged from Greek *ek*, meaning origin from, out and from Greek *poreuomai*, meaning to traverse, i.e. to travel) from the core of the spirit through self. Therefore, behavior comes out or is discharged from the spirit.

Perception of personal identity and self-image coincide with behavior. However, self-awareness does not predicate self determination. Nor should it be assumed that self awareness is a function of self determination. The men of Shechem were aware of the problem but did not retaliate until God sent the evil spirit upon them.

In Leviticus 20:27 another spirit is described as familiar (1 Samuel 28:7-8; 1 Chronicles 10:13; 2 Chronicles 33:6; Isa. 29:4). "A man or a woman who is a medium, or who has familiar spirits, shall surely be put to death; they shall stone them with stones. Their blood *shall be* upon them." A familiar (Hebrew *shawlome*, meaning safe) spirit (Hebrew *obe*, apparently meaning the idea of prattling a father's name. To prattle is to utter or make meaningless sounds suggestive of the chatter of children, i.e. babbling; trifling or empty talk; meaningless, and repetitive) returns to live within the spirit of life of the human being.

Jesus said spirits can return to the human being whereby they lived within the spirit of life (Luke 11:24-25). The affect of spirit within the spirit of life is to repeat the same experience as before. The behavior of a human being is repeated. The essence of the familiar spirit moves within as to affect the person's personality and cognitive interaction. The prattling of language does not suggest the spirit is young. Moreover since the spirit is a created being the dimension of time has no impeding result. The focus of affect is seated within the morphemes and semantics of language development whereby manipulation of time allows the familiar spirit to use receptive vocabulary for effect. Any person who has this familiar spirit would not be aware of its devices. Yet through reflection consider their life as a child with meaning and maturity.

In 1 Samuel 1:12-18 Hannah said she had a sorrowful spirit. Eli was watching Hannah as she prayed. "And it happened, as she continued praying before the Lord, that Eli watched her mouth. Now Hannah spoke in her heart; only her lips moved, but her voice was not heard. Therefore Eli thought she was drunk. So Eli said to her, "How long will you be drunk? Put your wine away from you!" And Hannah answered and said, "No, my lord, I *am* a woman of sorrowful spirit. I have drunk neither wine nor intoxicating drink, but have poured out my soul before the Lord. Do not consider your maidservant a wicked woman, for out of the abundance of my complaint and grief I have spoken until now." Then Eli answered and said, "Go in peace, and the God of Israel grant your petition which you have asked of Him." And she said, "Let your maidservant find favor in your sight." So the woman went her way and ate, and her face was no longer *sad*.

Hannah knew her spirit was sad. However, her own description of her behavior was similar to drunkenness. Eli thought Hannah had been drinking wine. As Hannah defended herself, she explained her behavior in spirit terms. Her spirit (Hebrew *ruah*) was sorrowful (Hebrew *qasheh*, meaning severe). Hannah described her actions were motivated by her spirit. Her belief about her life situation prompted further complaint and grief.

The severity of her anguish was observed as a lack of control of self. Eli assumed her behavior was attributed to drinking an intoxicating drink. The heightened level of emotion of Hannah was singly attributed to a spirit. Evidently Hannah was not aware when the spirit came into her spirit, but she was able to validate a significant level of complaining and grief. Her bitterness, anger, and continual crying consumed the focus of her emotions. The spirit moved her to try bargaining with God to bring change in her life.

In 1 Samuel 30:12 a man had not eaten for three days. After he had eaten his spirit came back to him again. "And they gave him a piece of a cake of figs, and two clusters of raisins: and when he had eaten, his spirit came again to him: for he had eaten no bread, nor drunk *any* water, three days and three nights." Is there a correlation between not eating food and the absence of spirit? Does the absence of spirit cause physiological weakness?

David and his men had become weary for chasing the Amalekites. Then they came upon an Egyptian in a field whom had not eaten for three days. After David's men gave him food, his spirit returned to him. The Hebrew word for Spirit is *ruah* meaning breath. This account also states the spirit came meaning to return back as transitive. Other translations (TEV, NKJV, NIV) have changed the word spirit for strength. Unfortunately, the Hebrew word does not mean strength or revived but spirit.

The same is true for Samson in Judges 15:19. After defeating the philistines with a jawbone of a donkey, Samson became very thirsty. God split open the ground and water came up. Samson drank the water and he revived. The description of spirit is the same in both instances. It was not the water that revived him physiologically but the spirit which revived him. It should not surprise you that a spirit being has effectual ability.

In 1 Kings 22:19-23 and 2 Chronicles 18:18-22 Micaiah warned Ahab. "And the king of Israel said to Jehoshaphat, "Did I not tell you he would not prophesy good concerning me, but evil?" Then *Micaiah* said, "Therefore hear the word of the Lord: I saw the Lord sitting on His throne, and all the host of heaven standing by, on His right hand and on His left. And the Lord said, 'Who will persuade (Hebrew *pata*, meaning to open i.e. causal make) Ahab to go up, that he may fall at Ramoth Gilead?' So one spoke in this manner, and another spoke in that manner. Then a spirit came (Hebrew *yasa*, meaning to go i.e. causatively bring, out) forward and stood before the Lord, and said, 'I will persuade him.' The Lord said to him, 'In what way?' So he said, 'I will go out and be a lying (Hebrew *sheqer*, meaning an untruth) spirit in the mouth of all his prophets.' And the Lord said, 'You shall persuade *him*, and also prevail (Hebrew *yakol*, meaning to be able). Go out and do so.' Therefore look! The Lord has put a lying spirit in the mouth of all these prophets of yours, and the Lord has declared disaster against you."

One spirit had affect upon Ahab and his prophets. This spirit was in heaven and volunteered to cause prophets to lie. The Lord in His sovereignty approved the "way" the spirit would move causing Ahab to believe the lie and his prophets to tell a lie. God's plan for Ahab was to die at Ramoth Gilead. This spirit left heaven and came into the spirit of each prophet. Each prophet would lie to King Ahab and morally lead him astray. The spirit caused each prophet to choose the lie. They were unable to not be in agreement.

The spirit persuaded each prophet from within their spirit with emotional and cognitive reciprocity. This is not the first time God has sent out a spirit to altercate the affairs of men (Judges 9:23; 1 Samuel 16:14; 18:10; 19:9; Job 12:16; Ezek. 14:9; 2 Thessalonians 2:11). The Hebrew language does not designate the spirits being good or evil. They are described as spirit. These spirits were in the hands of God. How large the hand of God must be. Moreover, how large is God?

Towns (2001) posited self direction is an expression of the heart. He quoted Johnson who said "the act of choice is in the heart, not in the brain (Romans 6:17, Exodus 35:21, 26, 29). When God sent the spirit into Ahab and his prophets, God told the spirit what the spirit was to do to them. Therefore, self direction and regulation are controlled by the indwelling essence of the spirit. The prophets did not have the control or regulated properties to alter the essence of the spirit.

In Nehemiah 9:20 the Lord sent a good spirit to instruct the people. The same spirit was in several men who would help Moses instruct the people (Numbers 11:16-30). It was not the intelligence, competence, age, gender, personality type, psychosocial skill or environmental effect that caused the men to be able to help Moses. Notice one spirit may be in more than one person, just as the Spirit of life is in every human being. And one spirit may be in many people and cause the same affect in human behavior affecting thought and reflection, perception, emotion, self-regulation and choice.

In Psalm 32:2 David describes a spirit as it may be deceitful. A deceitful spirit may attempt to reveal its essence as deceptive, misleading, not honest or playing tricks. The moral consciousness of a human being may be fully affected by the one spirit. The nature of every human being may be fully affected by this one spirit throughout each human life to not be honest or mislead. The universal moral depravity of every human being has a mind hostile on God (Romans 8:7-8).

At conception, the spirit in every baby includes a deceptive spirit (Genesis 6:5; 1 Kings 8:46; Psalm 14:1-3, 39:5; Jeremiah 17:9; Matthew 18:11; Mark 7:20-23; John 3:36; Romans 1:21; 2:1-29; 3:9-19; 8:7; 1 Corinthians 2:14; 2 Corinthians 3:14; 4:4; Galatians 5:19-21; Ephesians 2:1-3, 11-12; 4;18-22; Colossians 1:21; Hebrews 3:13; James 4:4). In human development a child begins to show behaviors exhibiting their sinful nature within months of birth. Michael Lewis (1995) studied the development of self conscious emotions such as pride, shame, guilt, and embarrassment that begin to appear after the infant's first birthday (Craig, Baucum, 2002).

Mele (1997) sighted Friedrich which suggested self-deception beliefs are the outcome of inappropriate and often egoistically driven processes. Overestimates of personal control could conceivable have negative consequences, but these are rarely evident in the designs of studies demonstrating "illusions of control." While Mele took another step suggesting self-deception is a logical extension of interpersonal deception. According to the Scriptures, self-deception has etiological causality by the deceptive spirit.

When a human being is deceitful, emotions may or may not be evidence revealing the affect. This spirit works independently from other spirits. It functions from the heart through cognition as a separate entity. The confliction of other spirits within the spirit of life arrive as emotion either regulated or non-regulated. Libet (1994) has shown that there is a delay of 0.5 seconds between the arrival of a stimulus and the onset of awareness of the stimulus.

In Psalm 34:18, a spirit may also cause a human to be humbled, or experience humility, emotional weakness, or emptiness. To experience a contrite (Hebrew *dakka,* meaning literally powder or crushed taken from the Hebrew *daka*, meaning to crumble) spirit is to have a crushed spirit. The crushing is a work of the spirit which affects other spirits within the spirit of life. To crush is to manage, manipulate, impede, hinder, or obstruct other spirits to bring about an emotional release causing new insight, self awareness, change of human will, mind focus, realignment of goals, self concept, etc.

Every human spirit will fall before God (Isaiah 57:15) i.e. to become feeble, weak, or enervated with decreasing self interest. Examples of psycho-physiological crushing of spirit may include depression, and grief. Since the heart is the core of emotions and conscience, the affect of the spirit is pervasive within cognitive process.

The Old Testament states it is God who gives human beings this spirit. Ezekiel 36:25-29 (NKJV) "Then I will sprinkle clean water on you, and you shall be clean; I will cleanse you from all your filthiness and from all your idols. I will give you a new heart and put a new spirit within you; I will take the heart of stone out of your flesh and give you a heart of flesh. I will put My Spirit within you and cause you to walk in My statutes, and you will keep My judgments and do *them.* Then you shall dwell in the land that I gave to your fathers; you shall be My people, and I will be your God. I will deliver you from all your uncleannesses. I will call for the grain and multiply it, and bring no famine upon you."

God gives and causes human beings to be contrite is their spirit. Such expression of emotional contrition is spiritual affect. The essence of this spirit is complete, full, motivates, empowers, dominates the human will, effect's the order of spirits within, has ranking authority, controls, impedes interpersonal relationships, impacting environmental influences and cultural cues.

In Psalm 51:10 a human being may also have a "right spirit." Psalm 51:10 (KJV) "Create in me a clean heart, O God; and renew a right spirit within me." To create (Hebrew *bara*, meaning to create) a clean (Hebrew *tahor*, meaning pure from *toher*, meaning to be bright) heart. The spirit will not have darkness within. Therefore, no dark spots will glow from within the spirit (John 12:36). A right (Hebrew *koon*, meaning to be erect, to establish, fix, apply, prepare) spirit in the human spirit is immediate transformation.

Does a renewed heart have affective properties which are reflective within emotional behavior? Does the removal of some spirits cause a right heart or is a right heart newly created? Is it possible that the removal of some spirits is the same as having a clean heart? Therefore, to create would be to cause removal and renew would be to have what was there before. The text does not imply God corrects the heart, but renews a right spirit. The renewed essence of the spirit in a human being would reveal express change of demeanor and temperament.

A right spirit would mirror the full essence of the spirit as explained in chapter one and two. A renewed spirit integrated within human developmental maturity. The hallmark of emotional maturity is not the ability to self-regulate in response to change and adaptation of experience. It is the bonding with God through unconditional love and acceptance in each emotion. The full essence of the right spirit is not a new ability to self-regulate throughout human development. That theory places the emphasis upon self, self-concept, and self-determination.

Then David said Psalm 51:12 (KJV) "Restore unto me the joy of thy salvation; and uphold me *with thy* free spirit." A free (Hebrew *Nadib,* meaning voluntary from Hebrew *nadab,* which means to impel) spirit urges or drives forward or on by or as if by the exertion of strong moral pressure; to impart motion. A right spirit is void of high emotional regulated release. A free spirit is not emotionally aggressive, haughty, loud, demanding, controlling of others, revengeful, retaliates, or shows partiality.

In Proverbs 16:19, 29:23; Isa. 57:15, the scriptures describe yet another spirit – a humble spirit. A humble (Hebrew *shapal,* meaning depressed, from Hebrew *shapel*, meaning to depress or sink i.e. to humiliate) spirit does not boast, exaggerate, draw attention to one-self or comparatively strive for possessions of others.

A prideful spirit dishonors (Proverbs 11:2), is destructive (Proverbs 16:18; 18:12), and is stumbling (Proverbs 16:18). A humble spirit is honorable (Proverbs 15:33; 18:12). This humility in the scriptures describe does not push in competitiveness but each spirit is without confliction thereby the human self-concept lacks forward resolve.

There are emotions which the humble spirit would not exasperate. Emotions like: abandonment, afraid, annoyed, anxious, ashamed, bashful, bewildered, confused, defeated, defensive, detached, disappointed, disgusted, distant, distrustful, disturbed, edgy, elated, embarrassed, enthusiastic, envy, expressive, fearful, foolish, frustrated, furious, guilty, helpless, hollow, hostile, hurt, inadequate, intense, irritable, jazzed, jealous, mean, miserable, neglected, nervous, outraged, pessimistic, pressured, prideful, puzzled, rejected, restless, revolted, sad, sensual, separated, shaky, shame, shy, silly, strong, tense, terrified, tired, trapped, ugly, uneasy, upset, uptight, used, vulnerable, weak or worried.

KEY WORDS

1. Affect of spirit
2. Behavior control
3. Deceptive spirit
4. Origination of behavior
5. Reciprocity of spirits
6. Self determination
7. Self direction
8. Spirit of Jealousy
9. Spirit of sorrow

KEY QUESTIONS

1. What can the spirit of Jealousy do in a human being?
2. Define emotional significance?
3. Does the human brain have origination of emotion centered within its neuronal subsystems?
4. Where does Jesus say origination of human behavior begins?
5. What is the affect of the spirit within the spirit of life?
6. Explain how a spirit has affective ability?
7. Explain how the affect of spirit is pervasive within cognitive process?

Quick Scripture Reference Guide

Genesis 6:5 (NKJV)

[5] Then the LORD saw that the wickedness of man *was* great in the earth, and *that* every intent of the thoughts of his heart *was* only evil continually.

Exodus 35:21 (NKJV)

[21] Then everyone came whose heart was stirred, and everyone whose spirit was willing, *and* they brought the LORD'S offering for the work of the tabernacle of meeting, for all its service, and for the holy garments.

Exodus 35:26 (NKJV)

[26] And all the women whose heart stirred with wisdom spun yarn of goats' *hair.*

Exodus 35:29 (NKJV)

[29] The children of Israel brought a freewill offering to the LORD, all the men and women whose hearts were willing to bring *material* for all kinds of work which the LORD, by the hand of Moses, had commanded to be done.

Leviticus 20:27 (NKJV)

[27] 'A man or a woman who is a medium, or who has familiar spirits, shall surely be put to death; they shall stone them with stones. Their blood *shall be* upon them.' "

Numbers 5:11-31 (NKJV)

[11] And the LORD spoke to Moses, saying,

[12] "Speak to the children of Israel, and say to them: 'If any man's wife goes astray and behaves unfaithfully toward him,

[13] and a man lies with her carnally, and it is hidden from the eyes of her husband, and it is concealed that she has defiled herself, and *there was* no witness against her, nor was she caught–

[14] if the spirit of jealousy comes upon him and he becomes jealous of his wife, who has defiled herself; or if the spirit of jealousy comes upon him and he becomes jealous of his wife, although she has not defiled herself–

[15] then the man shall bring his wife to the priest. He shall bring the offering required for her, one-tenth of an ephah of barley meal; he shall pour no oil on it and put no frankincense on it, because it *is* a grain offering of jealousy, an offering for remembering, for bringing iniquity to remembrance.

[16] 'And the priest shall bring her near, and set her before the LORD.

[17] The priest shall take holy water in an earthen vessel, and take some of the dust that is on the floor of the tabernacle and put *it* into the water.

[18] Then the priest shall stand the woman before the LORD, uncover the woman's head, and put the offering for remembering in her hands, which *is* the grain offering of jealousy. And the priest shall have in his hand the bitter water that brings a curse.

[19] And the priest shall put her under oath, and say to the woman, "If no man has lain with you, and if you have not gone astray to uncleanness *while* under your husband's *authority,* be free from this bitter water that brings a curse.

[20] But if you have gone astray *while* under your husband's *authority,* and if you have defiled yourself and some man other than your husband has lain with you"–

[21] then the priest shall put the woman under the oath of the curse, and he shall say to the woman–"the LORD make you a curse and an oath among your people, when the LORD makes your thigh rot and your belly swell;

[22] and may this water that causes the curse go into your stomach, and make *your* belly swell and *your* thigh rot." Then the woman shall say, "Amen, so be it."

[23] 'Then the priest shall write these curses in a book, and he shall scrape *them* off into the bitter water.

[24] And he shall make the woman drink the bitter water that brings a curse, and the water that brings the curse shall enter her *to become* bitter.

25 Then the priest shall take the grain offering of jealousy from the woman's hand, shall wave the offering before the LORD, and bring it to the altar;

26 and the priest shall take a handful of the offering, as its memorial portion, burn *it* on the altar, and afterward make the woman drink the water.

27 When he has made her drink the water, then it shall be, if she has defiled herself and behaved unfaithfully toward her husband, that the water that brings a curse will enter her *and become* bitter, and her belly will swell, her thigh will rot, and the woman will become a curse among her people.

28 But if the woman has not defiled herself, and is clean, then she shall be free and may conceive children.

29 'This *is* the law of jealousy, when a wife, *while* under her husband's *authority,* goes astray and defiles herself,

30 or when the spirit of jealousy comes upon a man, and he becomes jealous of his wife; then he shall stand the woman before the LORD, and the priest shall execute all this law upon her.

31 Then the man shall be free from iniquity, but that woman shall bear her guilt.' "

Numbers 14:29-30 (NKJV)

29 The carcasses of you who have complained against Me shall fall in this wilderness, all of you who were numbered, according to your entire number, from twenty years old and above.

30 Except for Caleb the son of Jephunneh and Joshua the son of Nun, you shall by no means enter the land which I swore I would make you dwell in.

Numbers 14:24 (NKJV)

24 But My servant Caleb, because he has a different spirit in him and has followed Me fully, I will bring into the land where he went, and his descendants shall inherit it.

Numbers 32:12 (NKJV)

[12] except Caleb the son of Jephunneh, the Kenizzite, and Joshua the son of Nun, for they have wholly followed the LORD.'

Judges 9:22-25 (NKJV)

[22] After Abimelech had reigned over Israel three years,

[23] God sent a spirit of ill will between Abimelech and the men of Shechem; and the men of Shechem dealt treacherously with Abimelech,

[24] that the crime *done* to the seventy sons of Jerubbaal might be settled and their blood be laid on Abimelech their brother, who killed them, and on the men of Shechem, who aided him in the killing of his brothers.

[25] And the men of Shechem set men in ambush against him on the tops of the mountains, and they robbed all who passed by them along that way; and it was told Abimelech.

Judges 15:19 (NKJV)

[19] So God split the hollow place that *is* in Lehi, and water came out, and he drank; and his spirit returned, and he revived. Therefore he called its name En Hakkore, which is in Lehi to this day.

Joshua 14:6-8 (NKJV)

[6] Then the children of Judah came to Joshua in Gilgal. And Caleb the son of Jephunneh the Kenizzite said to him: "You know the word which the LORD said to Moses the man of God concerning you and me in Kadesh Barnea.

[7] I *was* forty years old when Moses the servant of the LORD sent me from Kadesh Barnea to spy out the land, and I brought back word to him as *it was* in my heart.

[8] Nevertheless my brethren who went up with me made the heart of the people melt, but I wholly followed the LORD my God.

1 Samuel 1:12-18 (NKJV)

12 And it happened, as she continued praying before the LORD, that Eli watched her mouth.

13 Now Hannah spoke in her heart; only her lips moved, but her voice was not heard. Therefore Eli thought she was drunk.

14 So Eli said to her, "How long will you be drunk? Put your wine away from you!"

15 And Hannah answered and said, "No, my lord, I *am* a woman of sorrowful spirit. I have drunk neither wine nor intoxicating drink, but have poured out my soul before the LORD.

16 Do not consider your maidservant a wicked woman, for out of the abundance of my complaint and grief I have spoken until now."

17 Then Eli answered and said, "Go in peace, and the God of Israel grant your petition which you have asked of Him."

18 And she said, "Let your maidservant find favor in your sight." So the woman went her way and ate, and her face was no longer *sad*.

1 Samuel 16:14 (NKJV)

14 But the Spirit of the LORD departed from Saul, and a distressing spirit from the LORD troubled him.

1 Samuel 18:10 (NKJV)

10 And it happened on the next day that the distressing spirit from God came upon Saul, and he prophesied inside the house. So David played *music* with his hand, as at other times; but *there was* a spear in Saul's hand.

1 Samuel 19:9 (NKJV)

9 Now the distressing spirit from the LORD came upon Saul as he sat in his house with his spear in his hand. And David was playing *music* with *his* hand.

1 Samuel 28:7-8 (NKJV)

7 Then Saul said to his servants, "Find me a woman who is a medium, that I may go to her and inquire of her." And his servants said to him, "In fact, *there is* a woman who is a medium at En Dor."

8 So Saul disguised himself and put on other clothes, and he went, and two men with him; and they came to the woman by night. And he said, "Please conduct a seance for me, and bring up for me the one I shall name to you."

1 Samuel 30:12 (NKJV)

12 And they gave him a piece of a cake of figs and two clusters of raisins. So when he had eaten, his strength came back to him; for he had eaten no bread nor drunk water for three days and three nights.

1 Kings 8:46 (NKJV)

46 "When they sin against You (for *there is* no one who does not sin), and You become angry with them and deliver them to the enemy, and they take them captive to the land of the enemy, far or near;

1 Kings 22:19-23 (NKJV)

19 Then *Micaiah* said, "Therefore hear the word of the LORD: I saw the LORD sitting on His throne, and all the host of heaven standing by, on His right hand and on His left.

20 And the LORD said, 'Who will persuade Ahab to go up, that he may fall at Ramoth Gilead?' So one spoke in this manner, and another spoke in that manner.

21 Then a spirit came forward and stood before the LORD, and said, 'I will persuade him.'

22 The LORD said to him, 'In what way?' So he said, 'I will go out and be a lying spirit in the mouth of all his prophets.' And the LORD said, 'You shall persuade *him*, and also prevail. Go out and do so.'

[23] Therefore look! The LORD has put a lying spirit in the mouth of all these prophets of yours, and the LORD has declared disaster against you."

1 Chronicles 10:13 (NKJV)

[13] So Saul died for his unfaithfulness which he had committed against the LORD, because he did not keep the word of the LORD, and also because he consulted a medium for guidance.

2 Chronicles 18:18-22 (NKJV)

[18] Then *Micaiah* said, "Therefore hear the word of the LORD: I saw the LORD sitting on His throne, and all the host of heaven standing on His right hand and His left.

[19] And the LORD said, 'Who will persuade Ahab king of Israel to go up, that he may fall at Ramoth Gilead?' So one spoke in this manner, and another spoke in that manner.

[20] Then a spirit came forward and stood before the LORD, and said, 'I will persuade him.' The LORD said to him, 'In what way?'

[21] So he said, 'I will go out and be a lying spirit in the mouth of all his prophets.' And *the Lord* said, 'You shall persuade *him* and also prevail; go out and do so.'

[22] Therefore look! The LORD has put a lying spirit in the mouth of these prophets of yours, and the LORD has declared disaster against you."

2 Chronicles 33:6 (NKJV)

[6] Also he caused his sons to pass through the fire in the Valley of the Son of Hinnom; he practiced soothsaying, used witchcraft and sorcery, and consulted mediums and spiritists. He did much evil in the sight of the LORD, to provoke Him to anger.

Nehemiah 9:20 (NKJV)

[20] You also gave Your good Spirit to instruct them, And did not withhold Your manna from their mouth, And gave them water for their thirst.

Job 12:16 (NKJV)

[16] With Him *are* strength and prudence. The deceived and the deceiver *are* His.

Psalm 14:1-3 (NKJV)

[1] To the Chief Musician. A Psalm of David. The fool has said in his heart, "*There is* no God." They are corrupt, They have done abominable works, There is none who does good.

[2] The LORD looks down from heaven upon the children of men, To see if there are any who understand, who seek God.

[3] They have all turned aside, They have together become corrupt; *There is* none who does good, No, not one.

Psalm 32:2 (NKJV)

[2] Blessed *is* the man to whom the LORD does not impute iniquity, And in whose spirit *there is* no deceit.

Psalm 34:18 (NKJV)

[18] The LORD *is* near to those who have a broken heart, And saves such as have a contrite spirit.

Psalm 39:5 (NKJV)

[5] Indeed, You have made my days *as* handbreadths, And my age *is* as nothing before You; Certainly every man at his best state *is* but vapor. Selah

Psalm 51:10 (NKJV)

[10] Create in me a clean heart, O God, And renew a steadfast spirit within me.

Psalm 51:12 (NKJV)

[12] Restore to me the joy of Your salvation, And uphold me *by Your* generous Spirit.

Proverbs 11:2 (NKJV)

[2] When pride comes, then comes shame; But with the humble *is* wisdom.

Proverbs 15:33 (NKJV)

[33] The fear of the LORD *is* the instruction of wisdom, And before honor *is* humility.

Proverbs 16:18 (NKJV)

[18] Pride *goes* before destruction, And a haughty spirit before a fall.

Proverbs 16:19 (NKJV)

[19] Better *to be* of a humble spirit with the lowly, Than to divide the spoil with the proud.

Proverbs 18:12 (NKJV)

[12] Before destruction the heart of a man is haughty, And before honor *is* humility.

Proverbs 29:23 (NKJV)

[23] A man's pride will bring him low, But the humble in spirit will retain honor.

Proverbs 20:27 (NKJV)

[27] The spirit of a man *is* the lamp of the LORD, Searching all the inner depths of his heart.

Proverbs 25:28 (NKJV)

[28] Whoever *has* no rule over his own spirit *Is like* a city broken down, without walls.

Ecclesiastes 8:8 (NKJV)

[8] No one has power over the spirit to retain the spirit, And no one has power in the day of death. *There is* no release from that war, And wickedness will not deliver those who are given to it.

Isaiah 29:4 (NKJV)

[4] You shall be brought down, You shall speak out of the ground; Your speech shall be low, out of the dust; Your voice shall be like a medium's, out of the ground; And your speech shall whisper out of the dust.

Isaiah 38:16 (NKJV)

[16] O LORD, by these *things men* live; And in all these *things is* the life of my spirit; So You will restore me and make me live.

Isaiah 57:15 (NKJV)

[15] For thus says the High and Lofty One Who inhabits eternity, whose name *is* Holy: "I dwell in the high and holy *place,* With him *who* has a contrite and humble spirit, To revive the spirit of the humble, And to revive the heart of the contrite ones.

Jeremiah 17:9 (NKJV)

[9] "The heart *is* deceitful above all *things,* And desperately wicked; Who can know it?

Daniel 8:4 (NKJV)

[4] I saw the ram pushing westward, northward, and southward, so that no animal could withstand him; nor *was there any* that could deliver from his hand, but he did according to his will and became great.

Daniel 11:3 (NKJV)

[3] Then a mighty king shall arise, who shall rule with great dominion, and do according to his will.

Ezekiel 14:9 (NKJV)

[9] And if the prophet is induced to speak anything, I the LORD have induced that prophet, and I will stretch out My hand against him and destroy him from among My people Israel.

Ezekiel 36:25-29 (NKJV)

25 Then I will sprinkle clean water on you, and you shall be clean; I will cleanse you from all your filthiness and from all your idols.

26 I will give you a new heart and put a new spirit within you; I will take the heart of stone out of your flesh and give you a heart of flesh.

27 I will put My Spirit within you and cause you to walk in My statutes, and you will keep My judgments and do *them.*

28 Then you shall dwell in the land that I gave to your fathers; you shall be My people, and I will be your God.

29 I will deliver you from all your uncleannesses. I will call for the grain and multiply it, and bring no famine upon you.

Matthew 16:24-25 (NKJV)

24 Then Jesus said to His disciples, "If anyone desires to come after Me, let him deny himself, and take up his cross, and follow Me.

25 For whoever desires to save his life will lose it, but whoever loses his life for My sake will find it.

Matthew 18:11 (NKJV)

11 For the Son of Man has come to save that which was lost.

Mark 7:20-23 (NKJV)

20 And He said, "What comes out of a man, that defiles a man.

21 For from within, out of the heart of men, proceed evil thoughts, adulteries, fornications, murders,

22 thefts, covetousness, wickedness, deceit, lewdness, an evil eye, blasphemy, pride, foolishness.

23 All these evil things come from within and defile a man."

John 3:36 (NKJV)

[36] He who believes in the Son has everlasting life; and he who does not believe the Son shall not see life, but the wrath of God abides on him."

John 12:36 (NKJV)

[36] While you have the light, believe in the light, that you may become sons of light." These things Jesus spoke, and departed, and was hidden from them.

Romans 1:21 (NKJV)

[21] because, although they knew God, they did not glorify *Him* as God, nor were thankful, but became futile in their thoughts, and their foolish hearts were darkened.

Romans 2:1-29 (NKJV)

[1] Therefore you are inexcusable, O man, whoever you are who judge, for in whatever you judge another you condemn yourself; for you who judge practice the same things.

[2] But we know that the judgment of God is according to truth against those who practice such things.

[3] And do you think this, O man, you who judge those practicing such things, and doing the same, that you will escape the judgment of God?

[4] Or do you despise the riches of His goodness, forbearance, and longsuffering, not knowing that the goodness of God leads you to repentance?

[5] But in accordance with your hardness and your impenitent heart you are treasuring up for yourself wrath in the day of wrath and revelation of the righteous judgment of God,

[6] who *"will render to each one according to his deeds":*

[7] eternal life to those who by patient continuance in doing good seek for glory, honor, and immortality;

8 but to those who are self-seeking and do not obey the truth, but obey unrighteousness–indignation and wrath,

9 tribulation and anguish, on every soul of man who does evil, of the Jew first and also of the Greek;

10 but glory, honor, and peace to everyone who works what is good, to the Jew first and also to the Greek.

11 For there is no partiality with God.

12 For as many as have sinned without law will also perish without law, and as many as have sinned in the law will be judged by the law

13 (for not the hearers of the law *are* just in the sight of God, but the doers of the law will be justified;

14 for when Gentiles, who do not have the law, by nature do the things in the law, these, although not having the law, are a law to themselves,

15 who show the work of the law written in their hearts, their conscience also bearing witness, and between themselves *their* thoughts accusing or else excusing *them*)

16 in the day when God will judge the secrets of men by Jesus Christ, according to my gospel.

17 Indeed you are called a Jew, and rest on the law, and make your boast in God,

18 and know *His* will, and approve the things that are excellent, being instructed out of the law,

19 and are confident that you yourself are a guide to the blind, a light to those who are in darkness,

20 an instructor of the foolish, a teacher of babes, having the form of knowledge and truth in the law.

21 You, therefore, who teach another, do you not teach yourself? You who preach that a man should not steal, do you steal?

22 You who say, "Do not commit adultery," do you commit adultery? You who abhor idols, do you rob temples?

23 You who make your boast in the law, do you dishonor God through breaking the law?

24 For *"the name of God is blasphemed among the Gentiles because of you,"* as it is written.

25 For circumcision is indeed profitable if you keep the law; but if you are a breaker of the law, your circumcision has become uncircumcision.

26 Therefore, if an uncircumcised man keeps the righteous requirements of the law, will not his uncircumcision be counted as circumcision?

27 And will not the physically uncircumcised, if he fulfills the law, judge you who, *even* with *your* written *code* and circumcision, *are* a transgressor of the law?

28 For he is not a Jew who *is one* outwardly, nor *is* circumcision that which *is* outward in the flesh;

29 but *he is* a Jew who *is one* inwardly; and circumcision *is that* of the heart, in the Spirit, not in the letter; whose praise *is* not from men but from God.

Romans 3:9-19 (NKJV)

9 What then? Are we better *than they?* Not at all. For we have previously charged both Jews and Greeks that they are all under sin.

10 As it is written: *"There is none righteous, no, not one;*

11 *There is none who understands; There is none who seeks after God.*

12 *They have all turned aside; They have together become unprofitable; There is none who does good, no, not one."*

13 *"Their throat is an open tomb; With their tongues they have practiced deceit"; "The poison of asps is under their lips";*

[14] *"Whose mouth is full of cursing and bitterness."*

[15] *"Their feet are swift to shed blood;*

[16] *Destruction and misery are in their ways;*

[17] *And the way of peace they have not known."*

[18] *"There is no fear of God before their eyes."*

[19] Now we know that whatever the law says, it says to those who are under the law, that every mouth may be stopped, and all the world may become guilty before God.

Romans 6:17 (NKJV)

[17] But God be thanked that *though* you were slaves of sin, yet you obeyed from the heart that form of doctrine to which you were delivered.

Romans 8:7-8 (NKJV)

[7] Because the carnal mind *is* enmity against God; for it is not subject to the law of God, nor indeed can be.

[8] So then, those who are in the flesh cannot please God.

1 Corinthians 2:14 (NKJV)

[14] But the natural man does not receive the things of the Spirit of God, for they are foolishness to him; nor can he know *them*, because they are spiritually discerned.

2 Corinthians 3:14 (NKJV)

[14] But their minds were blinded. For until this day the same veil remains unlifted in the reading of the Old Testament, because the *veil* is taken away in Christ.

2 Corinthians 4:3-4 (NKJV)

[3] But even if our gospel is veiled, it is veiled to those who are perishing,

[4] whose minds the god of this age has blinded, who do not believe, lest the light of the gospel of the glory of Christ, who is the image of God, should shine on them.

Galatians 5:19-21 (NKJV)

[19] Now the works of the flesh are evident, which are: adultery, fornication, uncleanness, lewdness,

[20] idolatry, sorcery, hatred, contentions, jealousies, outbursts of wrath, selfish ambitions, dissensions, heresies,

[21] envy, murders, drunkenness, revelries, and the like; of which I tell you beforehand, just as I also told *you* in time past, that those who practice such things will not inherit the kingdom of God.

Ephesians 2:1-3 (NKJV)

[1] And you *He made alive,* who were dead in trespasses and sins,

[2] in which you once walked according to the course of this world, according to the prince of the power of the air, the spirit who now works in the sons of disobedience,

[3] among whom also we all once conducted ourselves in the lusts of our flesh, fulfilling the desires of the flesh and of the mind, and were by nature children of wrath, just as the others.

Ephesians 2:11-12 (NKJV)

[11] Therefore remember that you, once Gentiles in the flesh–who are called Uncircumcision by what is called the Circumcision made in the flesh by hands–

[12] that at that time you were without Christ, being aliens from the commonwealth of Israel and strangers from the covenants of promise, having no hope and without God in the world.

Ephesians 4:18-22 (NKJV)

[18] having their understanding darkened, being alienated from the life of God, because of the ignorance that is in them, because of the blindness of their heart;

19 who, being past feeling, have given themselves over to lewdness, to work all uncleanness with greediness.

20 But you have not so learned Christ,

21 if indeed you have heard Him and have been taught by Him, as the truth is in Jesus:

22 that you put off, concerning your former conduct, the old man which grows corrupt according to the deceitful lusts,

Colossians 1:21 (NKJV)

21 And you, who once were alienated and enemies in your mind by wicked works, yet now He has reconciled

2 Thessalonians 2:11 (NKJV)

11 And for this reason God will send them strong delusion, that they should believe the lie,

Hebrews 3:13 (NKJV)

13 but exhort one another daily, while it is called *"Today,"* lest any of you be hardened through the deceitfulness of sin.

James 4:4 (NKJV)

4 Adulterers and adulteresses! Do you not know that friendship with the world is enmity with God? Whoever therefore wants to be a friend of the world makes himself an enemy of God.

Chapter Seven – Definition of Emotional Terminology

In this chapter an alphabetized list of emotions and their terms are listed from the Merriam- Webster's Collegiate Dictionary, Eleventh Edition. This list is not conclusive moreover it does reveal a attempt to specify modern terminology of emotional words with their meanings. Some of the words have multiple meanings. So in this chapter the definitions describing feelings or emotions are added. Words in bold are not found in Christian Scriptures as searched in AMP; CEV; ESV; GW; NAB; NASB77; NASB; NCV; NIV; NJB; NKJV: NRSV; Phillips NT; TLB; TEV; but not limited to these as stated.

There are approximately 500 words used today that describe an array of human emotions and feelings. As you read through this list, you should look for feelings you have experienced and consider the level of emotion experienced. Using a 1-10 scale where 1 is the lowest and 10 is the greatest, you could specify the level of an emotion you have experienced. You might also consider which emotions you frequently experience and which emotions you have not.

A

Abandon – a thorough yielding to natural impulses
Abandoned – wholly free from restraint
Abandonment – a thorough yielding to impulses
Ablaze – radiant light or emotion with excitement
Accepted – to receive
Aching – causing or reflecting distress, emotion, or longing
Admirable – exciting wonder; surprising
Adore – to regard with loving admiration

Affection – a moderate feeling or emotion
Afflicted – to distress so severely as to cause persistent suffering or anguish
Affright – the sudden and great fear, terror
Afraid – filled with fear or apprehension
Aggravation – arousing displeasure, impatience, or anger
Agonize – to suffer agony, anguish
Agreeable – to be pleasing
Alarmed – a sudden sharp apprehension and fear resulting from the perception of imminent danger
Alone – being by oneself with slighter notion of emotional involvement, sadness and a sense of loss
Altruistic – unselfish regard for or devotion to the welfare of others
Amazed – to fill with wonder, bewildered, perplexed
Ambient – a feeling or mood associated with a particular place, person, or thing
Ambition – a desire to achieve a particular end
Ambivalence – simultaneous and contradictory attitudes or feelings toward an object, person, or action; a continual fluctuation
Anger – a strong feeling of displeasure
Angry – feeling or showing anger; wrathful
Angst – a feeling of anxiety, apprehension, or insecurity
Anguish – extreme distress or anxiety
Annoyed – the state or feeling of being disturbed or irritated
Antipathy – settled dislike; opposition in feeling
Antsy – restless, fidgety, impatient, eager, nervous, apprehensive
Anxiety – fearful concern or interest; an abnormal and over whelming sense of apprehension and fear
Anxious – extreme uneasiness of mind or brooding fear about some contingency; worried
Apathy – lack of feeling or emotion, Indifference
Appalling – inspiriting horror, dismay, or disgust
Appetency – a fixed and strong desire
Ardent – characterized by warmth of feeling expressed in eager, zealous support or activity
Ashamed – feeling shame, guilt, or disgrace; feeling inferior or unworthy
Astonished – to strike with sudden fear or great wonder or surprise
Astounded – to be overwhelmed with astonishment or amazement
Attachment – affectionate regard
Awful – afraid, terrified, extremely disagreeable or objectionable

B

Bashful – timid and shy
Belligerent – inclined to or exhibiting assertiveness, hostility, or compativeness
Bemoan – to express deep grief or distress; to regard with displeasure, disapproval or regret
Bewildered – to perplex or confuse by a complexity, variety or multitude of objects or considerations
Bitter – distasteful or distressing to the mind; marked by intensity or severity
Bittersweet – pleasure alloyed with pain; marked by elements of suffering or regret
Blah – a feeling of boredom, lethargy, or general dissatisfaction
Blessed – of or enjoying happiness
Boil – to be moved, excited, or stirred up
Boiling – an extreme degree – mad
Boil over – to become incensed as to lose one's temper
Boisterous – marked by or expressive of exuberance and high spirits
Bold – showing or requiring a fearless daring spirit
Boredom – the state of being weary and restless through lack of interest
Bound – something that limits or restrains
Brave – having or showing courage
Bright – lively, cheerful
Brittle – easily hurt or offended; sensitive
Broken – crushed, sorrowful
Brokenhearted – overcome by grief or despair
Brutal – grossly ruthless or unfeeling, very bad, unpleasant
Burden – something oppressive or worrisome
Burned out – worn out; exhausted
Burst – to give away from, an excess of emotion, to give vent suddenly to a repressed emotion

C

Cackle – to laugh especially in a harsh or sharp manner
Callosity – lack of feeling or capacity for emotion
Callous – being hardened and thickened
Calm – free from agitation, excitement, or disturbance
Care – to feel trouble or anxiety
Challenged – to arouse or stimulate especially by presenting with difficulties
Charged – possessing or showing strong emotion

Charitable – full of love for others
Charming – extremely pleasing or delightful
Cheap – contemptible because of lack of any fine, lofty, or redeeming qualities
Cheerful – full of good spirits
Chilly – lacking warmth of feeling
Chippy – aggressively belligerent
Cold – marked by a lack of warmth of normal human emotion, friendliness, or compassion
Collected – possessed of calmness and composure often through concentrated effort
Complacent – unconcerned
Compulsion – an irresistible persistent impulse to perform an act
Concern – an uneasy state of blended interest, uncertainty, and apprehension
Concerned – anxious, worried
Confidence – a feeling or consciousness of one's powers or of reliance on one's circumstances
Conflict – mental struggle resulting from incompatible or opposing needs, drives, wishes, or external or internal demands
Confused – being perplexed
Content – to appease the desires of; to limit oneself in requirements, desires, or actions
Covet – to feel inordinate desire for what belongs to another
Coward – one who shows disgraceful fear or timidity
Curious – marked by the desire to investigate and learn

D

Dead – incapable of being stirred emotionally or intellectually
Defeated – frustration
Defensive – devoted to resisting or preventing aggression
Defrauded – deprived of something by deception
Dejected – cast down in spirits; depressed, to make gloomy
Delight – a high degree of gratification; extreme satisfaction
Depressed – low in spirits
Derisive – expression to show contempt
Desire – too long or hope for; exhibit or feel desire for
Desolate – showing the effects of abandonment and neglect
Despair – to lose all hope or confidence
Desperate – having lost hope

Detached – standing by itself
Disappointed – defeated in expectation or hope
Disdain – a feeling of contempt for someone or something regarded as unworthy or inferior
Disgusted – to cause to lose an interest or intention
Disheartened – to cause to lose spirit or morale
Dishonored – to be shamed
Dismay – to cause to lose courage or resolution; upset
Dissension – disagreement
Distress – a painful situation; to cause to worry or be troubled
Distressful – causing distress
Disturbed – showing symptoms of emotional illness
Divided – disagreeing with each other
Dolorous – causing, marked by, or expressing misery or grief
Doormat – one that submits without protest to abuse or indignities
Downhearted – downcast, dejected
Drab – characterized by dullness
Dread – great fear in the face of impending evil; extreme uneasiness in the face of a disagreeable prospect
Dreary – feeling, displaying, or reflecting listlessness or discouragement

E

Eager – marked by enthusiastic or impatient desire or interest
Ecstasy – a state of being beyond reason and self-control
Edge – intensity of desire or enjoyment
Effusion – unrestrained expression of words or feelings
Elated – marked by high spirits
Embarrass – to cause to experience a state of self-conscious distress
Emotion – a state of feeling, a conscious mental reaction subjectively experienced as strong feeling usually directed toward a specific object and typically accompanied by physiological and behavioral changes in the body
Emotional – dominated by or prone to emotion
Emotionless – showing, having or expressing no emotion
Empathy – the action of understanding, being aware of, being sensitive to, and vicariously experiencing the feelings, thoughts, and experience of another of either the past or present without having the feelings, thoughts, and experience fully communicated in an objectively explicit manner
Empty – containing nothing

Emulous – inspired by or deriving from a desire to emulate; jealous
Engagement – emotional involvement or commitment
Enjoy – to take pleasure or satisfaction in
Enmity – positive, active, and typically mutual hatred or ill will
Enthuse – to make enthusiastic
Enthusiasm – strong excitement of feeling
Enthusiastic – filled with or marked by enthusiasm
Envious – feeling or showing envy
Envy – painful or resentful awareness of an advantage enjoyed by another joined with a desire to possess the same advantage
Excitable – capable of being readily roused into action or a state of excitement or irritability
Excite – to rouse to an emotional response
Exhilarate – to make cheerful and excited
Express – to give or convey a true impression; to make known the opinions or feelings of oneself
Exuberant – joyously unrestrained and enthusiastic

F

Faint-hearted – lacking courage, timid
Fastidious – reflecting a meticulous, sensitive, or demanding attitude
Fear – to be afraid of; a reverential awe of God; an unpleasant often strong emotion caused by anticipation or awareness of danger
Fearful – causing or likely to cause fear, fright or alarm
Fervent – exhibiting or marked by great intensity of feeling
Fervor – intensity of feeling or expression
Fond – to lavish affection; desirous
Foolish – lacking in sense, judgment, or discretion
Forbearance – patience
Fraught – causing or characterized by emotional distress or tension
Free – relieved from or lacking something unpleasant or burdensome
Fret – to cause to suffer emotional strain
Fright – fear excited by sudden danger
Frigid – lacking warmth, indifferent
Frost – to make angry or irritated
Frustrate – to induce feelings of discouragement
Frustration – a deep chronic sense of insecurity and dissatisfaction arising from unresolved problems or unfulfilled needs
Furious – giving a stormy appearance; exhibited by anger

G

Gentle – kind, amiable, soft
Ghastly – intensely unpleasant, disagreeable or objectionable
Giddy – lightheartedly silly, joyfully elated
Glad – experiencing pleasure, joy, or delight
Glee – exultant high spirited joy
Gloomy – lacking in promise or hopefulness
Glum – dreary, gloomy
Golly – to express surprise
Gracious – pleasing, accepting, kindness, courtesy
Grateful – appreciative of benefits received
Grief – deep and poignant distress caused by or as if by bereavement
Grievous – causing or characterized by severe pain, suffering, or sorrow
Grouchy – given to grumbling, a fit of bad temper
Grudge – to be unwilling to give or admit, a feeling of deep-seated resentment or ill will
Guilty – aware of or suffering from guilt, feelings of culpability especially for imagined offenses or from a sense of inadequacy

H

Happiness - a state of well-being and contentment
Happy - enjoying or characterized by well-being or contentment
Hard - bitterness or grief
Hard-headed - stubborn, willful
Hard Hearted - lacking in sympathetic understanding, unfeeling
Harsh - causing a disagreeable or painful sensory reaction, irritating
Hate - intense hostility and aversion, usually deriving from fear, anger, or sense of injury
Hateful - full of hate, malicious
Hatred - hate, prejudiced hostility or animosity
Haughty - blatantly and disdainfully proud
Heartbroken - overcome by sorrow
Heavy - hard to bear, grievous, afflictive
Helpless - marked by an inability to act or react, not able to be controlled or restrained
High - filled with or expressing great joy of excitement
Hollow - lacking in real value, sincerity, or substance, false, meaningless

Hope - to cherish a desire with anticipation
Hopeless - having no expectation of good or success, despairing
Hostile - openly opposed or resisting
Hot - violent, stormy, angry, eager, zealous
Hot-blood - one having strong passions or a quick temper
Humble - not proud or haughty, not arrogant or assertive
Humiliate - to reduce to a lower position in one's own eyes or others eyes
Humiliating - destructive to one's self-respect or dignity
Hurt - to cause emotional pain or anguish, to offend
Hurtful - causing injury, detriment, or suffering
Hypocrite - a person who acts in contradiction to his or her stated beliefs or feelings
Hysteria - behavior exhibiting overwhelming or unmanageable fear or emotional excess
Hysterics - a fit of uncontrollable laughter or crying

I

Ignore - to refuse to take notice of
Ill - with displeasure or hostility
Impassion - to arouse feelings or passions of
Impassioned - filled with passion or zeal, warmth or intensity of feeling
Impassive - destitute of emotion
Impel - to urge or drive forward or on by, or as if by the exertion of strong moral pressure, force
Impetuous - marked by impulsive vehemence or passion
Impressive - having the power to excite attention, awe, or admiration
Inadequate - not adequate, insufficient
Incongruous - not harmonious, not conforming, disagreeing
Incurious - lacking a normal or usual curiosity, uninterested
Indifferent - marked by impartiality, marked by no special liking for or dislike of something
Indurate - to make unfeeling, stubborn, or obdurate
Ineffable - incapable of being expressed in words, indescribable
Inefficacious - lacking the power to produce a desired effect, ineffective
Inefficacy - lack of power to produce a desired effect
Insecure - not confident or sure
Insensible - lacking emotional response, apathetic, indifferent
Insensitive - lacking feeling or tact

Intense - marked by or expressive of great zeal, energy, determination, concentration; exhibiting strong feelings or earnestness of purpose
Intimacy - the state of being intimate, familiarity
Intimidate - to make timid or fearful
Intolerable - not tolerable, unbearable
Intolerant - unable or unwilling to endure matters
Inviolable - secure from violation or profanation
Irritate - to provoke impatience, anger, or displeasure in
Irritative - serving to excite
Isolated - occurring alone or once
Isolation - the action of isolation, the condition of being isolated

J

Jangle - to quarrel verbally, noisy quarreling
Jealous - intolerant of rivalry or unfaithfulness
Jitter - a sense of panic or extreme nervousness, to be nervous or act in a nervous way
Joy - the emotion evoked by well-being, success, or good fortune or by the prospect of
possessing what one desires, to experience great pleasure or delight
Jubilant - exultant
Jubilate - rejoice
Juiced - full of energy and motivation

K

Kind - affectionate, loving
Kindless - disagreeable
Kindly - pleasant

L

Languish - to be or become feeble, weak, to be or live in a state of depression or decreasing vitality, to become dispirited
Lazy - sluggish
Lonely - being without company; lone

Lonesome - sad or dejected as a result of, lack of companionship or separation from others
Longing - a strong desire especially for something unattainable, craving
Loss - the harm or privation resulting from loss or separation
Lost - lacking assurance or self-confidence
Love - strong affection for another
Low - down-deeply emotional, blues
Lower - to look sullen, frown, to reduce in value
Lowly - humble in manner or spirit
Lumpish - low in spirits
Lyricism - an intense personal quality expressive of feeling or emotion in an art

M

Mad - completely unrestrained by reason and judgment, carried away by intense anger, furious, carried away by enthusiasm or desire
Malice - desire to cause pain, injury, or distress to another
Malign - evil in nature, influence, or effect, injurious
Mania - excitement manifested by mental and physical hyperactivity, disorganization of behavior and elevation of mood
Maniac - madman, lunatic, a person characterized by an inordinate or ungovernable enthusiasm for something
Mean - characterized by petty, selfishness or malice, causing trouble or bother, vexatious
Mean spirited - exhibiting or characterized by meanness of spirit
Meek - enduring injury with patience and without resentment, deficient in spirit and courage
Melancholic - depressed
Melancholy -characterized by irascibility or depression
Mellow - pleasant, agreeable
Merciful - full of mercy, compassionate
Merciless - having or showing no mercy
Mercy - compassion or forbearance shown, especially to an offender or to one subject to one's power
Merry - full of gaiety or high spirits
Mischief - action that annoys or irritates
Mischievous - able or tending to cause annoyance, trouble, or minor injury
Mood - a conscious state of mind or predominant emotion, feeling
Moody - subject to depression, gloomy

Mournful - expressing sorrow, full of sorrow
Moving - stirring deeply in a way that evokes a strong emotional response

N

Needed - to be needful or necessary, to be in want
Needless - not needed, unnecessary
Needy - being in want
Neglect - to give little attention or respect to, disregard
Neglectful - given to neglecting
Nervous - easily excited or irritated
Nervous breakdown - an attack of mental or emotional disorder, especially when of sufficient severity to require hospitalization
Nervy - showing or expressive of calm courage
Nettle - to arouse to sharp but transitory annoyance or anger
Nettled – aroused to sharp but transitory annoyance or anger
Neurosis - mental and emotional disorder that affects only part of the personality
Nice - polite, kind
Nuisance - one that is annoying, unpleasant, or obnoxious

O

Obdurate – stubbornly persistent in wrongdoing, hardened in feelings
Obsession - a persistent disturbing preoccupation with an often unreasonable idea or feeling
Offense - something that outrages the moral or physical senses
Offensive - giving painful or unpleasant sensations, causing displeasure or resentment
Opacity - the quality or state of being mentally obtuse, dullness
Open - exposed or vulnerable to attack or question
Oppress – to crush, burden by abuse of power or authority, to burden spiritually or mentally
Oppression - a sense of being weighted down in body or mind, depression
Oppressive - unreasonably burdensome or severe, overwhelming or depressing to the spirit or senses
Outrage - the anger and resentment aroused by injury or insult
Outraged - to arouse anger or resentment in, usually by some grave offense
Outrageous - going beyond all standards of what is right or decent
Overbear – to bring down by superior weight or force, overwhelm

Overbearing - to bring down by excessive weight or force, overwhelm
Over determined - excessively determined
Over pressure - pressure significantly above what is usual or normal
Overwhelm – to overcome by superior force or numbers, to overpower in thought or feeling
Overwhelming - tending or serving to overwhelm, force

P

Pacify - to allay the anger or agitation of, soothe
Pain - acute mental or emotional distress or suffering, grief, to make suffer or cause distress to, hurt
Pained - feeling pain, hurt
Painful - feeling or giving pain
Panic - relating to or resembling the mental or emotional state believed induced by the god Pan, a sudden overpowering fright, acute extreme anxiety, sudden unreasoning terror often accompanied by mass flight
Passion -emotion, intense driving or overmastering feeling or conviction, a strong liking or desire for or devotion to some activity, object, or concept
Passionate - easily aroused to anger, filled with anger, capable of, affected by, or expressing intense feeling
Patience - the capacity, habit, or fact of being patient
Patient - bearing pains or trials calmly or without complaint
Peaceable - disposed to peace, not contentious or quarrelsome, quietly behaved, marked by freedom from strife or disorder
Peaceful - untroubled by conflict, agitation, or commotion, quiet, tranquil
Pessimistic - relating to, or characterized by pessimism
Pitiful - deserving or arousing pity or commiseration
Pitiless - harsh, cruel
Pity - capacity to feel pity, something to be regretted
Playful - humorous, jocular
Pleasance - a feeling of pleasure, delight
Pleasant - having qualities that tend to give pleasure or satisfaction
Please - to afford, or give pleasure or satisfaction
Pleasing - giving pleasure, agreeable
Pleasurable -pleasant, gratifying
Pleasure - desire, inclination
Poignant - painfully affecting the feelings, piercing
Pressure - the burden of physical or mental distress

Pressured - to apply pressure
Pride - to indulge
Prideful - disdainful, haughty, exultant, elated
Protective - to cover or shield from exposure, injury, damage, or destruction
Proud - feeling or showing pride
Proud hearted - haughty
Prurient - marked by or arousing an immoderate or unwholesome interest or desire, marked by arousing or appealing to sexual desires
Pungent - poignant, suggests something is sharply or piercingly effective in stirring one's emotions
Put down - degrade, belittle, criticize, humiliate
Puzzled - to be uncertain as to action or choice
Puzzle headed - having or based on confused attitudes or ideas

Q

Quiet - gentle, easygoing, enjoyed in peace and relaxation, unobtrusive

R

Raddled - being in a state of confusion
Radiant - marked by or expressive of love, confidence or happiness
Regret - to be very sorry for, sorrow aroused by circumstances beyond one's control or power to repair, an expression of distressing emotion
Reject - to refuse to accept, consider, submit to, take for some purpose, or use
Reject - one rejected as not wanted, unsatisfactory, or not fulfilling standard requirements
Relaxed - freed from or lacking in precision or stringency, set or being at rest or ease
Release - to relieve from something that confines, burdens, or oppresses
Released - to be relieved from something that confines, burdens, or oppresses
Relieved - experiencing or showing relief, especially from anxiety or pent up emotions
Restless - characterized by, or manifesting unrest, especially of mind
Revenge - a desire for revenge, an act or instance of retaliating in order to get even
Revolt - to experience disgust or shock
Revolting - extremely offensive behavior
Ridicule - to make fun of
Ridiculous - arousing or deserving ridicule
Rotten - morally corrupt, extremely unpleasant or inferior, very uncomfortable

Rundown - worn out, exhausted
Rush - a surging of emotion

S

Sad - affected with or expressive of grief or unhappiness, downcast, causing or associated with grief or unhappiness, depressing
Safe - secure from threat of danger, harm, or loss
Sarcastic - mean, marked by bitterness and a power or will to cut or sting
Satiate - to satisfy (as a need or desire) fully or to excess
Secretive - not open or outgoing in speech, activity, or purpose
Secure - easy in mind, confident, assured in opinion or expectation, having no doubt, free from danger, free from risk of loss
Self abandonment - a surrender of one's selfish interests or desires
Sensitive - easily hurt or damaged, easily hurt emotionally
Sensual - relating to or consisting in the gratification of the senses or the indulgence of appetite, fleshly
Sensualistic - persistent or excessive pursuit of sensual pleasures and interests
Sensuous - producing or characterized by gratification of the senses, having strong sensory appeal, pleasure
Sentience - feeling or sensation as distinguished from perception and thought
Sentimental - marked or governed by feeling, sensibility, or emotional idealism
Sentimentality - the quality or state of being sentimental, especially to excess or in affection
Separated - to set or keep apart
Shaky - likely to give way or break down
Shallow - lacking in depth of knowledge, thought, or feeling
Shame - a painful emotion caused by consciousness of guilt, short coming, or impropriety, a condition of humiliating disgrace or disrepute
Shameful - bring shame, disgraceful, arousing the feeling of shame, full of the feeling of shame, ashamed
Shock - sudden or violent mental or emotional disturbance
Shun - Shunned-to avoid deliberately and especially habitually
Shy - easily frightened, timid
Silly - exhibiting or indicative of a lack of common sense or sound judgment
Sore head - a person easily angered or disgruntled
Sorrow - deep distress, sadness, or regret, especially for the loss of someone or something loved, resultant unhappy or unpleasant state

Stable - firmly established, fixed, steadfast, not subject to insecurity or emotional illness, sane, rational
Stilly -in a calm manner, quietly
Strife - bitter sometimes violent conflict or dissension
Strong - extreme, intense, not easily injured or disturbed, solid, not easily upset or nauseated
Stupendous - causing astonishment or wonder
Stupid - dulled in feeling or sensation
Subdued - lacking in vitality, intensity or strength
Suffocating – ending or serving to suffocate or overpower, overwhelming
Sullen - gloomily or resentfully silent or repressed
Super heated - exceedingly emotional or intense
Surprise - the state of being surprised, astonishment

T

Temper - state of feeling or frame of mind at a particular time, usually dominated by a single strong emotion, heat of mind or emotion, proneness to anger
Temperamental - marked by excessive sensitivity and impulsive mood changes
Temperance - moderation in action, thought, or feeling, restraint
Tender - highly susceptible to impressions or emotions, impressionable
Tender hearted - easily moved to love, pity, or sorrow, compassionate, impressionable
Tense - feeling or showing nervous tension
Tension - inner striving, unrest, or imbalance often with physiological indication of emotion
Terrible - exciting extreme alarm or intense fear
Terrify - to fill with terror
Terror - a state of intense fear
Thankful - expressive of thanks
Thankless - not expressing or feeling gratitude
Threatened - to cause to feel insecure or anxious
Ticked - angry, upset
Tight - marked by unusual tension
Timid - lacking in courage or self-confidence
Timorous - of a timid disposition, fearful
Tolerant - marked by forbearance or endurance
Torment - extreme pain or anguish of body or mind, agony, to cause severe, usually persistent or recurrent distress of body or mind

Torture - anguish of body or mind, agony, the infliction of intense pain, to punish, coerce, or afford sadistic pleasure
Tortured - to cause intense suffering to, torment
Torturous - very unpleasant or painful
Tranquil - free from agitation of mind or spirit
Trap - a position or situation from which it is difficult or impossible to escape
Trash - inferior or worthless
Trouble - to agitate mentally or spiritually, worry, disturb, a cause of distress, annoyance or inconvenience
Troubled - concerned, worried
Tuckered - exhaust

U

Ugly - offensive or unpleasant to any sense, likely to cause inconvenience or discomfort
Unacceptable - not pleasing or welcome
Unashamed - not ashamed, being without guilt, self-consciousness, or doubt
Uneasy - causing physical or mental discomfort, marked by lack of ease, awkward, embarrassed, apprehensive, worried, restless, unquiet
Unemotional - not easily aroused or excited, cold, involving a minimum of emotion, intellectual
Ungenerous - petty, mean, deficient in liberality
Ungrateful - showing non gratitude
Unkind – not pleasing or mild, lacking in kindness or sympathy
Unlovely - disagreeable, unpleasant
Unmerciful - not merciful, merciless, excessive, extreme
Unquiet - not quiet, agitated, turbulent, physically, emotionally, or mentally restless, uneasy
Unrelenting - not softening or yielding to determination, hard, stern, not letting up or weakening in vigor or pace, constant
Unselfish - not selfish, generous
Unsettle - to perturb or agitate mentally or emotionally
Unsettled - not calm or tranquil, disturbed
Upbeat - cheerful, optimistic
Uppity - putting on airs of superiority, arrogant, presumptuous
Uptight - being tense, nervous, or uneasy, angry, indignant
Urgency - a force or impulse that impels or constrains
Used - availing oneself of something as an means or instrument to an end

V

Vain - having no real value, idle, worthless
Valid - being at once relevant or meaningful
Valuable - having desirable or esteemed characteristics or qualities
Vent - to give often vigorous or emotional expression to, to relieve by means of a vent, an opportunity or means of escape, passage, or release, outlet
Verve - the spirit and enthusiasm animating artistic composition or performance, energy, vitality
Vibrant - responsive, sensitive
Vicious - marked by violence or ferocity, fierce
Victim - one that is subjected to oppression, hardship, or mistreatment
Victorious - evincing moral harmony or a sense of fulfillment
Vigorous - possessing vigor, full of physical or mental strength or active force, strong
Vindicative - vengeful
Violent - extreme, intense, emotionally agitated to the point of loss of self-control
Void - useless, a feeling of want or hollowness
Voluptuous - full of delight or pleasure to the senses, conductive to or rising from sensuous or sensual gratification
Vulnerable - capable of being physically or emotionally wounded

W

Wallow - to roll oneself about in a lazy, relaxed or ungainly manner
Want - to desire to come, go, or be, to have a strong desire for, something wanted, need, desire
Wanting - not being up to standards or expectations
Warm – feeling or causing sensations of heat brought about by strenuous exertion, comfortably established, secure, marked by strong feelings, ardent, marked by excitement, disagreement or anger, to infuse with a feeling of love, friendship, well-being, or pleasure, to fill with anger, zeal, or passion
Weaken - to reduce in intensity or effectiveness
Weakness - the quality or state or being weak
Weary - exhausted in strength, endurance, or freshness, expressing or characteristic of weariness, having one's patience, tolerance or pleasure exhausted
Well being - the state of being happy, healthy, or prosperous
Wicked - morally very bad, evil, disposed to or marked by mischief, roguish, disgustingly unpleasant, causing or likely to cause harm, distress, or trouble

Wild - emotionally overcome, indicative of strong passion, desire, or emotion
Wish - to have a desire for, to have a desire, want
Wishful - expressive of a wish, hopeful, having a wish, desirous
Wishy washy – lacking in character or determination, ineffectual
Withdrawn - socially detached and unresponsive, exhibiting withdrawal, introverted
Wonder - a cause of astonishment or admiration, rapt attention or astonishment at something awesomely mysterious or new to one's experience, a feeling of doubt or uncertainty
Wondered - to feel surprised, to feel curiosity or doubt
Wonderful - exciting wonder
Worry - mental distress or agitation resulting from concern, usually for something impending or anticipated, anxiety, an instance or occurrence of such distress or agitation
Worst - most unfavorable, difficult, unpleasant, or painful
Worthless - lacking worth, valueless, useless
Wounded - injured, hurt by, or suffering from a wound, feelings
Wrath - strong vengeful anger or indignation
Wrathful - filled with wrath
Wreak - to give free play or course to malevolent feeling, bring about, cause, havoc
Wronged - to treat disrespectfully or dishonorably

X

Y

Yucky - repugnant, distasteful, unpleasant, disagreeable

Z

Zeal - eagerness and ardent interest in pursuit of something, fervor
Zingy - enjoyably exciting

Chapter Eight – Emotion Regulation

MY GOAL IN THIS CHAPTER is to provide a theological map on emotional regulation. To specify the process through theological terminology and citation of scripture on how emotion is regulated. Since I accept the authority of scripture as absolute I will not speculate, or theorize my own postulations.

Gross posited emotional regulation refers to how we try to influence which emotions we have, when we have them, and how we experience and express them. Hall and Lindzey (1957) suggested they are beneficial for adjustment. Kottler and Brown (2000) quoted Ellis which suggested emotional regulation was a choice, due to years of lazy negligence and wallowing in our irrational beliefs, to interpret the world negatively and consequently to feel depressed, anxious, guilty, or frustrated.

Gulliland and James (1998) explained people largely create their own emotional disturbances. Because people have a measure of self-determination, they can choose to indoctrinate themselves in disturbed or undisturbed ways. Rational emotive behavior theorists believe people have the power to change their self-defeating habits, but such change requires actively working at modifying thoughts, behaviors, and feelings. They agreed with Ellis that inherent change is hedonism predicated on a scientific and empirical, rather than a mystical, devoutly religious, or external, locus of control. Hall (et. al.) agreed stating the intensity of the emotion varies according to the meaning the situation has to the person.

Sharf (2000) noticed in family systems theory, the higher the level of anxiety and emotional dependence, the more likely children are to experience an emotional cutoff in a family. Gross and Thompson (et.al., 2008) suggested people themselves regulate their own negative or positive emotions either by decreasing or increasing them. Quirk (2008) placed the responsibility for inhibiting subcortical areas that generate prepotent responses to conditioned stimuli.

Beer and Lombardo (2008) put the focus on human experience in which we may automatically or more deliberately attend to information, events, and people that make us feel good and avoid or ignore those who evoke negative emotions. Second, once an emotional experience has arisen, we may manipulate the magnitude of our response in order to quickly suppress negative emotions and amplify or perpetuate positive emotions.

In the following, Sperry (1995) designates the emotional regulatory action within Personality Disorders.

ANTISOCIAL PERSONALITY DISORDER

Emotional style is characterized as shallow and superficial. They avoid "softer" emotions such as warmth and intimacy.

AVOIDANT PERSONALITY DISORDER

Emotional style is marked by a shy and apprehensive quality. Because they are seldom able to obtain unconditional approval from others, they routinely experience sadness, loneliness, and tenseness.

BORDERLINE PERSONALITY DISORDER

Emotional style is marked by mood shifts from a normal or euthymic mood to a dysphoric mood. Inappropriate and intense anger and rage may be easily triggered. At other extreme are feelings of emptiness, a deep "void" or boredom.

DEPENDENT PERSONALITY DISORDER

Emotional style is characterized by insecurity and anxiousness. Because they lack self-confidence, they experience considerable discomfort at being alone. They tend to be preoccupied with the fear of abandonment and of the disapproval of others.

HISTRIONIC PERSONALITY DISORDER

Emotional style is characterized by exaggerated emotional displays and excitability, including irrational outbursts and temper tantrums. Although they are constantly seeking reassurance that they are loved, they respond with only superficial warmth and charm and are generally emotionally shallow.

NARCISSISTIC PERSONALITY DISORDER

Emotional style is characterized toward others which vacillate between over idealization and devaluation. Their inability to show empathy is reflected in their superficial relationships, with minimal emotional ties or commitments.

OBSESSIVE-COMPULSIVE DISORDER

Emotional style is characterized as grim and cheerless. They have difficulty with expressing intimate feelings such as warmth and tenderness, tending to avoid the "softer" feelings, although they may exhibit anger, frustration, and irritability quite freely.

PARANOID PERSONALITY DISORDER

Emotional style is characterized as cold, aloof, unemotional, and humorless. They lack a deep sense of affection, warmth, and sentimentality. The two emotions they express in some depth are anger and intense jealousy.

PASSIVE-AGGRESSIVE PERSONALITY DISORDER

Emotionally passive –aggressive individuals do not show anger directly, but instead tend to sulk and become sullen. Although temper tantrums were common in them as children, temper outbursts are rarely seen in the passive-aggressive adult.

SCHIZOID PERSONALITY DISORDER

Emotional style is characterized as humorless, cold, aloof, and unemotional. They appear to be indifferent to praise and criticism and they lack spontaneity. Their rapport and ability to empathize with others are poor. They have a constricted range of affective response.

SCHIZOTYPAL PERSONALITY DISORDER

Their affective style is described as cold, aloof, and unemotional, with constricted affect. They are humorless and difficult to engage in conversation, probably because of their general suspicious and mistrustful nature. They are hypersensitive to real or imagined slights.

Within the science of Psychology theorists have set some presuppositions as to how human beings regulate their own emotions. Such as human beings can regulate their own emotion; emotional disturbances are psychopathological; and regulation is self-determined. These presuppositions are scaffold in nature built upon observable empirical research which bases its supporting evidence on data, many experiences, on demonstrations, and on facts (Berger, 2008).

My theological presuppositions are scripture supported. Towns (2001) said a presupposition is a conclusion that is not arrived at on the basis of any reason, experience, or demonstrated proof. Therefore, it is a "self-evident truth". He uses five tests to determine a presupposition as truth.

First, is the test of consistency asking, "Is the system consistent?" Second, is the test of correspondence asking, "Does it correspond to reality or life?" A system of theology may be a consistent doctrinal system which does not correspond with truth found in natural revelation. Third, is the test of priority of data, discriminating between what is essential and what is irrelevant. The important data will become foremost in your theology and that which is less important will fall to the rear of your thinking. The fourth test, is the test of cohesiveness, you determine the cohesive nature of the data. Is the data cohesive with every doctrine in scripture. And fifth, is the test of thoroughness. This test is a rigorous examination of any and all questions related to the topic. This is an attempt to answer all inquiries regarding a system of belief. To ignore or omit any question regarding any subject matter is to have a theology that is not complete and comprehensive.

My presuppositions are theologically posited upon Scripture. First, that there is one God and He created man. Second, that God put the spirit of life in every human being. Third, that emotion in man is constituted from the spirit of life in man. Fourth, that each spirit regulates emotion in each human being from what the spirit sees. And fifth, no human being has regulatory control over his spirit.

Already in previous chapters these presuppositions have been tested and documented as fact. By resolving the issues of presuppositions from theory to fact, the next step is to specify the theological terminology which supports the presuppositions as stated above.

In Job 9:18, Job said God *fills* (Hebrew *saba*, meaning to sate, to fill to satisfaction) me with bitterness. In Lamentations 3:15, the prophet said "He (God) has filled me with bitterness" (Romans 3:14). In Esther 5:9, Haman was full (Hebrew *mala*, meaning to fill) of indignation against Mordecai. Others were full of fury (Isa. 51:20; Jer. 6:11; Dan. 3:19). Some were full of compassion (Psalm 78:38, 86:15, 111:4, 145:8); full of deceit (Jer. 5:27); full of violence (Eze. 7:23); full of perverseness (Eze. 9:9); full of wrath (Acts 19:28; Revelation 15:7); and full of envy, murder, debate, and evil mindedness (Romans 1:29).

In several scriptures, emotion is *lit* in human beings (Gen. 30:2; Num. 11:1, 22:27, 24:10; Judges 9:30, 14:19; 1 Samuel 11:6, 17:28, 20:30; 2 Samuel 12:5; Job 32:2-5). In other scriptures God's emotion is *lit* within him (Num. 11:33, 12:9, 22:22, 25:3, 32:10, 32;13; Deuteronomy 6:15, 7:4, 11:17, 29:27; Joshua 7:1, 23:16; 2 Samuel 6:7, 24:1; 2 Kings 13:3, 22:13, 23:26; 1 Chronicles 13:10; 2 Chronicles 25:15; Job 42:7; Psalm 106:40; Isa. 5:25).

One question to ask is does God do the lighting or does the lighting of emotion have etiological significance in the neuronal pathogens in the human brain? Scripture states the lighting of emotion in the human spirit is kindled by God (Psalm 2:12; Jeremiah 15:14, 17:4, 21:14; Eze. 20:47-48; Hosea 8:5).

Another word describes the *kindling* of spirit and that is 'aflame' (Hebrew *lahat,* meaning to blaze or set on fire and *yatsath,* meaning to kindle). These scriptures state God sets the means to which human spirits blaze with emotion (Proverbs 29:8; Isa. 50:11; Job 15:30). "To kindle" is to increase the intensity of what the spirit sees (Genesis 39:19; Deuteronomy 11:17; 2 Kings 22:17; Job 19:11, 32:2-5, 42:7; Psalm 2:12, 106:40, 124:3).

In 2 Kings 19:7, God said He would blast Sennacherib, king of Assyria. *Blast* is the Hebrew *ruah,* which means spirit. Blast signifies the affect of emotion whereby partial regulation was manifested by the spirit. Adrammelech and Sharezer struck their father with a sword. The same spirit moved Sennacherib to worship in the temple of Nisroch, his god while the spirit moved his sons with strong emotion to kill their father.

Valenced movement by the spirit, within the spirit of life of a human being, makes use of human personality without error or excess within conscious experience. Sennacherib was moved to be in the right place to hear a rumor causing him to fear. Sennacherib spent time in the temple of Nisroch worshipping his god, the Assyrian god of agriculture (Isa. 37:38).

To blast also reveals the power of the spirit over dimension (Exodus 15:8), physical objects (Joshua 6:5), human experience (2 Samuel 22:16), human death (Job 4:9; Isa. 37:36), and emotional and physical strength (Isa. 25:4). Notice the absence of human regulation of emotion yet, humanly speaking Adrammelech and Sharezer must have felt passionately about killing their father. The planning, timing, preparation for an assassination would have taken considerable thought process. Moreover, scripture does not say Adrammelech and Sharezer knew a spirit was working within them to bring about this human death and escape to Ararat. The absence of spiritual knowledge cascades empirical research suggesting emotional regulation as a psychosocial domain.

In 2 Chronicles 36:15-21, a new term describes the same spirit in God which moved His anger. "And the LORD God of their fathers sent to them by his messengers, rising up betimes, and sending; because he had compassion on his people, and on his dwelling place: But they mocked the messengers of God, and despised his words, and misused his prophets, *until the wrath of the LORD arose against his people,* till *there was* no remedy. Therefore he brought upon them the king of the Chaldees, who slew their young men with the sword in the house of their sanctuary, and had no compassion upon young man or maiden, old man, or him that stooped for age: he gave *them* all into his hand. And all the vessels of the house of God, great and small, and the treasures of the house of the LORD, and the treasures of the king, and of his princes; all *these* he brought to Babylon. And they burnt the house of God, and brake down the wall of Jerusalem, and burnt all the palaces thereof with fire, and destroyed all the goodly vessels thereof. And them that had escaped from the sword carried he away to Babylon; where they were servants to him and his sons until the reign of the kingdom of Persia: To fulfil the word of the LORD by the mouth of Jeremiah, until the land had enjoyed her sabbaths: *for* as long as she lay desolate she kept sabbath, to fulfil threescore and ten years.

When the Lord's anger *arose* (Hebrew *ala,* meaning to ascend) there was no remedy. His anger arose which moved him to motivate a king to kill many men. This ascending of emotion in the Spirit of God is equal to the scriptural data which posited that each spirit regulates in each human being from what the spirit sees.

When a spirit comes (Ephesians 5:6, Colossians 3:6) and brings a level of emotion to become behavior it may come slow (Proverbs 14:29; James 1:19), heap up (Job 36:13), be past (Job 14:13), turn away (2 Chronicles 12:12, 30:8; Proverbs 15:1, 29:8; Jeremiah 18:20 [Hebrew *anaph,* meaning to breath hard i.e. stop breathing hard from strong emotion]), or brought low (Job 14:21; Psalm 79:8; 106:43; 107:12; 116:6). The spirit turns away from seeing and therefore the strong emotional physiological behavior ceases. The intensity level may be full (Esther 3:5; Acts 19:28), strong (Proverbs 21:14) or fierce (Ezra 10:14).

KEY WORDS

1. Emotional regulation
2. Emotional style
3. Kindling of spirit
4. Test of cohesiveness
5. Test of consistency
6. Test of correspondence
7. Test of thoroughness
8. Test of priority of data
9. Valenced movement of spirit

KEY QUESTIONS

1. Explain how emotion in human beings is regulated?
2. How is emotion lit in human beings?
3. What can a kindling spirit do in a human being?
4. How does a spirit regulate emotion in a human being?

Quick Scripture Reference Guide

Genesis 30:2 (NKJV)

2 And Jacob's anger was aroused against Rachel, and he said, "*Am* I in the place of God, who has withheld from you the fruit of the womb?"

Genesis 39:19 (NKJV)

19 So it was, when his master heard the words which his wife spoke to him, saying, "Your servant did to me after this manner," that his anger was aroused.

Exodus 15:8 (NKJV)

8 And with the blast of Your nostrils The waters were gathered together; The floods stood upright like a heap; The depths congealed in the heart of the sea.

Numbers 11:1 (NKJV)

1 Now *when* the people complained, it displeased the LORD; for the LORD heard *it,* and His anger was aroused. So the fire of the LORD burned among them, and consumed *some* in the outskirts of the camp.

Numbers 11:33 (NKJV)

33 But while the meat *was* still between their teeth, before it was chewed, the wrath of the LORD was aroused against the people, and the LORD struck the people with a very great plague.

Numbers 12:9 (NKJV)

9 So the anger of the LORD was aroused against them, and He departed.

Numbers 22:22 (NKJV)

22 Then God's anger was aroused because he went, and the Angel of the LORD took His stand in the way as an adversary against him. And he was riding on his donkey, and his two servants *were* with him.

Numbers 22:27 (NKJV)

[27] And when the donkey saw the Angel of the LORD, she lay down under Balaam; so Balaam's anger was aroused, and he struck the donkey with his staff.

Numbers 24:10 (NKJV)

[10] Then Balak's anger was aroused against Balaam, and he struck his hands together; and Balak said to Balaam, "I called you to curse my enemies, and look, you have bountifully blessed *them* these three times!

Numbers 25:3 (NKJV)

[3] So Israel was joined to Baal of Peor, and the anger of the LORD was aroused against Israel.

Numbers 32:10 (NKJV)

[10] So the LORD'S anger was aroused on that day, and He swore an oath, saying,

Numbers 32:13 (NKJV)

[13] So the LORD'S anger was aroused against Israel, and He made them wander in the wilderness forty years, until all the generation that had done evil in the sight of the LORD was gone.

Deuteronomy 6:15 (NKJV)

[15] (for the LORD your God *is* a jealous God among you), lest the anger of the LORD your God be aroused against you and destroy you from the face of the earth.

Deuteronomy 7:4 (NKJV)

[4] For they will turn your sons away from following Me, to serve other gods; so the anger of the LORD will be aroused against you and destroy you suddenly.

Deuteronomy 11:17 (NKJV)

[17] lest the LORD'S anger be aroused against you, and He shut up the heavens so that there be no rain, and the land yield no produce, and you perish quickly from the good land which the LORD is giving you.

Deuteronomy 29:27 (NKJV)

[27] Then the anger of the LORD was aroused against this land, to bring on it every curse that is written in this book.

Joshua 6:5 (NKJV)

[5] It shall come to pass, when they make a long *blast* with the ram's horn, *and* when you hear the sound of the trumpet, that all the people shall shout with a great shout; then the wall of the city will fall down flat. And the people shall go up every man straight before him."

Joshua 7:1 (NKJV)

[1] But the children of Israel committed a trespass regarding the accursed things, for Achan the son of Carmi, the son of Zabdi, the son of Zerah, of the tribe of Judah, took of the accursed things; so the anger of the LORD burned against the children of Israel.

Joshua 23:16 (NKJV)

[16] When you have transgressed the covenant of the LORD your God, which He commanded you, and have gone and served other gods, and bowed down to them, then the anger of the LORD will burn against you, and you shall perish quickly from the good land which He has given you."

Judges 9:30 (NKJV)

[30] When Zebul, the ruler of the city, heard the words of Gaal the son of Ebed, his anger was aroused.

Judges 14:19 (NKJV)

[19] Then the Spirit of the LORD came upon him mightily, and he went down to Ashkelon and killed thirty of their men, took their apparel, and gave the changes *of clothing* to those who had explained the riddle. So his anger was aroused, and he went back up to his father's house.

1 Samuel 11:5-6 (NKJV)

[5] Now there was Saul, coming behind the herd from the field; and Saul said, "What *troubles* the people, that they weep?" And they told him the words of the men of Jabesh.

[6] Then the Spirit of God came upon Saul when he heard this news, and his anger was greatly aroused.

1 Samuel 17:28 (NKJV)

[28] Now Eliab his oldest brother heard when he spoke to the men; and Eliab's anger was aroused against David, and he said, "Why did you come down here? And with whom have you left those few sheep in the wilderness? I know your pride and the insolence of your heart, for you have come down to see the battle."

1 Samuel 20:30 (NKJV)

[30] Then Saul's anger was aroused against Jonathan, and he said to him, "You son of a perverse, rebellious *woman!* Do I not know that you have chosen the son of Jesse to your own shame and to the shame of your mother's nakedness?

2 Samuel 6:7 (NKJV)

[7] Then the anger of the LORD was aroused against Uzzah, and God struck him there for *his* error; and he died there by the ark of God.

2 Samuel 12:5 (NKJV)

[5] So David's anger was greatly aroused against the man, and he said to Nathan, "*As* the LORD lives, the man who has done this shall surely die!

2 Samuel 24:1 (NKJV)

1 Again the anger of the LORD was aroused against Israel, and He moved David against them to say, "Go, number Israel and Judah."

2 Samuel 22:16 (NKJV)

16 Then the channels of the sea were seen, The foundations of the world were uncovered, At the rebuke of the LORD, At the blast of the breath of His nostrils.

2 Kings 13:3 (NKJV)

3 Then the anger of the LORD was aroused against Israel, and He delivered them into the hand of Hazael king of Syria, and into the hand of Ben-Hadad the son of Hazael, all *their* days.

2 Kings 19:7 (NKJV)

7 Surely I will send a spirit upon him, and he shall hear a rumor and return to his own land; and I will cause him to fall by the sword in his own land." ' "

2 Kings 22:13 (NKJV)

13 "Go, inquire of the LORD for me, for the people and for all Judah, concerning the words of this book that has been found; for great *is* the wrath of the LORD that is aroused against us, because our fathers have not obeyed the words of this book, to do according to all that is written concerning us."

2 Kings 22:17 (NKJV)

17 because they have forsaken Me and burned incense to other gods, that they might provoke Me to anger with all the works of their hands. Therefore My wrath shall be aroused against this place and shall not be quenched.' " '

2 Kings 23:26 (NKJV)

26 Nevertheless the LORD did not turn from the fierceness of His great wrath, with which His anger was aroused against Judah, because of all the provocations with which Manasseh had provoked Him.

1 Chronicles 13:10 (NKJV)

10 Then the anger of the LORD was aroused against Uzza, and He struck him because he put his hand to the ark; and he died there before God.

2 Chronicles 12:12 (NKJV)

12 When he humbled himself, the wrath of the LORD turned from him, so as not to destroy *him* completely; and things also went well in Judah.

2 Chronicles 30:8 (NKJV)

8 Now do not be stiff-necked, as your fathers *were, but* yield yourselves to the LORD; and enter His sanctuary, which He has sanctified forever, and serve the LORD your God, that the fierceness of His wrath may turn away from you.

2 Chronicles 25:15 (NKJV)

15 Therefore the anger of the LORD was aroused against Amaziah, and He sent him a prophet who said to him, "Why have you sought the gods of the people, which could not rescue their own people from your hand?"

2 Chronicles 36:15-21 (NKJV)

15 And the LORD God of their fathers sent *warnings* to them by His messengers, rising up early and sending *them,* because He had compassion on His people and on His dwelling place.

16 But they mocked the messengers of God, despised His words, and scoffed at His prophets, until the wrath of the LORD arose against His people, till *there was* no remedy.

17 Therefore He brought against them the king of the Chaldeans, who killed their young men with the sword in the house of their sanctuary, and had no compassion on young man or virgin, on the aged or the weak; He gave *them* all into his hand.

18 And all the articles from the house of God, great and small, the treasures of the house of the LORD, and the treasures of the king and of his leaders, all *these* he took to Babylon.

[19] Then they burned the house of God, broke down the wall of Jerusalem, burned all its palaces with fire, and destroyed all its precious possessions.

[20] And those who escaped from the sword he carried away to Babylon, where they became servants to him and his sons until the rule of the kingdom of Persia,

[21] to fulfill the word of the LORD by the mouth of Jeremiah, until the land had enjoyed her Sabbaths. As long as she lay desolate she kept Sabbath, to fulfill seventy years.

Ezra 10:14 (NKJV)

[14] Please, let the leaders of our entire assembly stand; and let all those in our cities who have taken pagan wives come at appointed times, together with the elders and judges of their cities, until the fierce wrath of our God is turned away from us in this matter."

Esther 3:5 (NKJV)

[5] When Haman saw that Mordecai did not bow or pay him homage, Haman was filled with wrath.

Esther 5:9 (NKJV)

[9] So Haman went out that day joyful and with a glad heart; but when Haman saw Mordecai in the king's gate, and that he did not stand or tremble before him, he was filled with indignation against Mordecai.

Job 4:9 (NKJV)

[9] By the blast of God they perish, And by the breath of His anger they are consumed.

Job 9:18 (NKJV)

[18] He will not allow me to catch my breath, But fills me with bitterness.

Job 14:13 (NKJV)

[13] "Oh, that You would hide me in the grave, That You would conceal me until Your wrath is past, That You would appoint me a set time, and remember me!

Job 14:21 (NKJV)

21 His sons come to honor, and he does not know *it;* They are brought low, and he does not perceive *it.*

Job 15:30 (NKJV)

30 He will not depart from darkness; The flame will dry out his branches, And by the breath of His mouth he will go away.

Job 19:11 (NKJV)

11 He has also kindled His wrath against me, And He counts me as *one of* His enemies.

Job 32:2-5 (NKJV)

2 Then the wrath of Elihu, the son of Barachel the Buzite, of the family of Ram, was aroused against Job; his wrath was aroused because he justified himself rather than God.

3 Also against his three friends his wrath was aroused, because they had found no answer, and *yet* had condemned Job.

4 Now because they *were* years older than he, Elihu had waited to speak to Job.

5 When Elihu saw that *there was* no answer in the mouth of these three men, his wrath was aroused.

Job 36:13 (NKJV)

13 "But the hypocrites in heart store up wrath; They do not cry for help when He binds them.

Job 42:7 (NKJV)

7 And so it was, after the LORD had spoken these words to Job, that the LORD said to Eliphaz the Temanite, "My wrath is aroused against you and your two friends, for you have not spoken of Me *what is* right, as My servant Job *has.*

Psalm 2:12 (NKJV)

[12] Kiss the Son, lest He be angry, And you perish *in* the way, When His wrath is kindled but a little. Blessed *are* all those who put their trust in Him.

Psalm 78:38 (NKJV)

[38] But He, *being* full of compassion, forgave *their* iniquity, And did not destroy *them.* Yes, many a time He turned His anger away, And did not stir up all His wrath;

Psalm 79:8 (NKJV)

[8] Oh, do not remember former iniquities against us! Let Your tender mercies come speedily to meet us, For we have been brought very low.

Psalm 86:15 (NKJV)

[15] But You, O Lord, *are* a God full of compassion, and gracious, Longsuffering and abundant in mercy and truth.

Psalm 106:40 (NKJV)

[40] Therefore the wrath of the LORD was kindled against His people, So that He abhorred His own inheritance.

Psalm 106:43 (NKJV)

[43] Many times He delivered them; But they rebelled in their counsel, And were brought low for their iniquity.

Psalm 107:12 (NKJV)

[12] Therefore He brought down their heart with labor; They fell down, and *there was* none to help.

Psalm 111:4 (NKJV)

[4] He has made His wonderful works to be remembered; The LORD *is* gracious and full of compassion.

Psalm 116:6 (NKJV)

[6] The LORD preserves the simple; I was brought low, and He saved me.

Psalm 124:3 (NKJV)

[3] Then they would have swallowed us alive, When their wrath was kindled against us;

Psalm 145:8 (NKJV)

[8] The LORD *is* gracious and full of compassion, Slow to anger and great in mercy.

Proverbs 14:29 (NKJV)

[29] *He who is* slow to wrath has great understanding, But *he who is* impulsive exalts folly.

Proverbs 15:1 (NKJV)

[1] A soft answer turns away wrath, But a harsh word stirs up anger.

Proverbs 21:14 (NKJV)

[14] A gift in secret pacifies anger, And a bribe behind the back, strong wrath.

Proverbs 29:8 (NKJV)

[8] Scoffers set a city aflame, But wise *men* turn away wrath.

Isaiah 5:25 (NKJV)

[25] Therefore the anger of the LORD is aroused against His people; He has stretched out His hand against them And stricken them, And the hills trembled. Their carcasses *were* as refuse in the midst of the streets. For all this His anger is not turned away, But His hand *is* stretched out still.

Isaiah 25:4 (NKJV)

[4] For You have been a strength to the poor, A strength to the needy in his distress, A refuge from the storm, A shade from the heat; For the blast of the terrible ones *is* as a storm *against* the wall.

Isaiah 37:36 (NKJV)

[36] Then the angel of the LORD went out, and killed in the camp of the Assyrians one hundred and eighty-five thousand; and when *people* arose early in the morning, there were the corpses–all dead.

Isaiah 37:38 (NKJV)

[38] Now it came to pass, as he was worshiping in the house of Nisroch his god, that his sons Adrammelech and Sharezer struck him down with the sword; and they escaped into the land of Ararat. Then Esarhaddon his son reigned in his place.

Isaiah 50:11 (NKJV)

[11] Look, all you who kindle a fire, Who encircle *yourselves* with sparks: Walk in the light of your fire and in the sparks you have kindled– This you shall have from My hand: You shall lie down in torment.

Isaiah 51:20 (NKJV)

[20] Your sons have fainted, They lie at the head of all the streets, Like an antelope in a net; They are full of the fury of the LORD, The rebuke of your God.

Jeremiah 5:27 (NKJV)

[27] As a cage is full of birds, So their houses *are* full of deceit. Therefore they have become great and grown rich.

Jeremiah 6:11 (NKJV)

[11] Therefore I am full of the fury of the LORD. I am weary of holding *it* in. "I will pour it out on the children outside, And on the assembly of young men together; For even the husband shall be taken with the wife, The aged with *him who is* full of days.

Jeremiah 15:14 (NKJV)

[14] And I will make *you* cross over with your enemies Into a land *which* you do not know; For a fire is kindled in My anger, *Which* shall burn upon you."

Jeremiah 17:4 (NKJV)

[4] And you, even yourself, Shall let go of your heritage which I gave you; And I will cause you to serve your enemies In the land which you do not know; For you have kindled a fire in My anger *which* shall burn forever."

Jeremiah 18:20 (NKJV)

[20] Shall evil be repaid for good? For they have dug a pit for my life. Remember that I stood before You To speak good for them, To turn away Your wrath from them.

Jeremiah 21:14 (NKJV)

[14] But I will punish you according to the fruit of your doings," says the LORD; "I will kindle a fire in its forest, And it shall devour all things around it." ' "

Lamentations 3:15 (NKJV)

[15] He has filled me with bitterness, He has made me drink wormwood.

Ezekiel 7:23 (NKJV)

[3] 'Make a chain, For the land is filled with crimes of blood, And the city is full of violence.

Ezekiel 9:9 (NKJV)

[9] Then He said to me, "The iniquity of the house of Israel and Judah *is* exceedingly great, and the land is full of bloodshed, and the city full of perversity; for they say, 'The LORD has forsaken the land, and the LORD does not see!'

Ezekiel 20:47-48 (NKJV)

47 and say to the forest of the South, 'Hear the word of the LORD! Thus says the Lord GOD: "Behold, I will kindle a fire in you, and it shall devour every green tree and every dry tree in you; the blazing flame shall not be quenched, and all faces from the south to the north shall be scorched by it.

48 All flesh shall see that I, the LORD, have kindled it; it shall not be quenched."

Daniel 3:19 (NKJV)

19 Then Nebuchadnezzar was full of fury, and the expression on his face changed toward Shadrach, Meshach, and Abed-Nego. He spoke and commanded that they heat the furnace seven times more than it was usually heated.

Hosea 8:5 (NKJV)

5 Your calf is rejected, O Samaria! My anger is aroused against them– How long until they attain to innocence?

Romans 1:29 (NKJV)

29 being filled with all unrighteousness, sexual immorality, wickedness, covetousness, maliciousness; full of envy, murder, strife, deceit, evil-mindedness; *they are* whisperers,

Romans 3:14 (NKJV)

14 *"Whose mouth is full of cursing and bitterness."*

Acts 19:28 (NKJV)

28 Now when they heard *this,* they were full of wrath and cried out, saying, "Great *is* Diana of the Ephesians!"

Ephesians 5:6 (NKJV)

6 Let no one deceive you with empty words, for because of these things the wrath of God comes upon the sons of disobedience.

Colossians 3:6 (NKJV)

6 Because of these things the wrath of God is coming upon the sons of disobedience,

James 1:19 (NKJV)

19 So then, my beloved brethren, let every man be swift to hear, slow to speak, slow to wrath;

Revelation 15:7 (NKJV)

7 Then one of the four living creatures gave to the seven angels seven golden bowls full of the wrath of God who lives forever and ever.

Chapter Nine – The Role of Emotion in Feeling

LARSON, BERNTSON, POEHLMANN, ITO AND Cacioppo (2008) posited the experience of emotions (i.e. feelings) cause peripheral changes. Such changes send and receive input through the central nervous system and viscera. Solomon (2008) called feelings "affect and inner sensation". Frijda (2008) suggested feelings express states of mind to others.

Tooby and Cosmides (2008) developed their own hypothesis of feelings. They said "we think that they are usually nonconscious or implicit. Outputs of processes that access these variables may be consciously experienced. We think that it may be possible eventually to arrive at a precise description of computational understructure subserving the world of feeling, by considering feeling to be a special form of computation that evolved to deal with the world of valuation." Panksepp (2008) viewed feelings as arising from cognitive readout of the unconscious emotional commotions of the body.

In this chapter, feeling of emotion is "in the bringing". The spirit of life in each human being brings them up to "see". Moreover, when the spirit "sees" through the human eye, said feeling is reality of experience. Feelings are not originated in the brain and then throughout the central nervous system. Johnson-Laird and Oatley (2008) postulated emotions arise from unconscious transitions.

In fact, the scriptures state feelings in human beings are the same as in Jesus Christ (Philippians 1:8; Hebrews 2:18, 4:15) from his heart. The same spirit of life in Jesus Christ is equal to the spirit of life in each human being. As stated in early chapters, the spirit in each human being is from God.

The human eye lid does not have to be open for the minds' eye to "see". Like dreaming is to sleeping so the feelings are to awareness of self. Since feeling comes from the movement of the spirit, the spirit is regulating human action. A good example of this is 2 Kings 22. Micaiah saw God, discussing with spirits, His plan for Ahab and asked which spirit would fulfill His divine plan. The spirit moved an entire group of men to avenge Ahab.

Freudian psychology describes a dualistic nature of the mind as conscious and unconscious. He further stated the unconscious is an actual entity of the mind, the lowest of its three layers. It stores material that is unavailable to awareness because of incompatibility (Gilliland, James, 1998; Kittler, Brown, 2000). Jung believed the unconscious contained forgotten or repressed material that has been lost to conscious thought but is still retrievable. The unconscious is the transpersonal or non-personal conscious that is not concerned with any personal experiences.

Jung hypothesized the self is the regulating center of personality and mediates between conscious, unconscious, and collective unconscious. The self is at the center core which is the unifying and stabilizing agent of the personality. Notice both Jung and Freud developed a psychology without theological underpinnings. That which is at the core of a human being is spirit. The spirit fully encompasses the soul which is physiologically manifested. Without the spirit no human being would have feeling or emotion.

Jung also believed the unconscious was not concerned with any personal experience. We now know this is incorrect. First, there is no unconscious, moreover, there is spirit which brings cognitive process through the spirits mind's eye. Second, the spirit is interested and regulates personal experiences in each human being. Third, self is not at the center core unifying and stabilizing personality. The spirit of life may have a multiplicity of spirits coming and leaving which is effectual to human experience.

An entire psychological theory of unconsciousness has been built upon a hypothesized framework which is theologically incorrect. Even Glasser thought the brain was central to feeling origination. Glasser stated human beings are not passive, determined responders, but actors pursuing desired ends. The brain creates an inner image of external reality and then acts in accord with that inner image to meet needs. Thus the factors that shape behavior are primarily the nature of the inner image, the action capabilities the person has available, and expectations based on the past track record for how the various behavioral options have worked out (Jones, Butman, 1991).

Gilliland and Jones (et. al) believed people create their own emotional disturbance. Because people have a measure of self-determination, they can choose to indoctrinate themselves in disturbed or undisturbed ways. They sighted Ellis who suggested children become emotionally disturbed not only because of parental attitudes toward them, but also because of the own tendency to take these attitudes too seriously, to internalize them, and to perpetuate them through the years. He posited it is one's belief system that leads to inappropriate emotional consequences such as rage, depression, and extreme anxiety. I have already proved this is theologically unfounded.

Ellis clearly stated nobody or nothing outside of ourselves can cause us to feel anything. There is no bad-temper button on our foreheads that anyone else can push to make us angry on demand. Granted, many things that people do or events that occur are highly conducive to letting us upset ourselves. Nevertheless, it is our choice, due to years of lazy negligence and wallowing in our irrational beliefs, to interpret the world negatively and consequently to feel depressed, anxious, guilty, or frustrated (Kottler, et. al). Albert Ellis was incorrect. He believed thoughts determine emotional reaction. His presuppositions of rigid structures in psychoanalysis establishing the ABC theory of emotions is theologically unfounded.

When a spirit brings up feelings, is the spirit regulating the human experience by valence? Does the spirit bring feelings from cognitive readout of the unconscious emotional commotions of the body (Panksepp, 2008)? Are modern cortical readout theories of emotions overarching claims of the importance of amygdale?

Panksepp (et. al) chose to disregard the diverse affective aspects of the "law of effect" because they raised the specter of scientifically unobservable internal processes – apparent nonmaterial principles – within the brain. In fact, the very internal processes are needed to make sense of emotions and feelings. Without a theological explanation of the nonmaterial principles, scientific observation will not be able to explain affect of emotion.

To better understand how feelings regulate human experience, several passages of scripture will be discussed. Each spirit is always true to its purpose of habitation within the spirit of life in each human being. Affective valence in bringing of feeling constitutes a human experience with or without observance from others. Each human experience is degreed manifestation. Therefore, the scientific means of observing human behavior to delineate the valence of feeling has no fundamental merit.

By what measure do spirits determine a specific velocity of bringing to affect human experience? When the Lord asked a spirit to persuade Ahab to go up to Ramoth Gilead (1 Kings 22:19-40), three spirits offered different means. The mean or manner is the Hebrew word *koh,* means to open up. It was up to each spirit to bring feelings within Ahab which motivated his cognitive process to consider going up to Ramoth Gilead.

The purpose of God is sovereign (1 Chronicles 29:11; Daniel 4:35; Psalms 115:3, 22:8) and the chosen spirit to employ God's purpose in each human being is regulated within the spirit of life for each human experience. After the affirmation from God to employ by persuasion, God said "the spirit would persuade and prevail, go out and do so" (verse 22). To prevail is from the Hebrew *yakol,* meaning to be able. This spirit was given permission to specifically "bring" the necessary movement within Ahab so that he would die at Ramoth Gilead.

In Judges 9:22-57, God sent a spirit of ill will between Abimelech and the men of Shechem. The purpose was to settle the crime against the seventy sons of Jerubbaal and requiring their blood be laid upon Abimelech who killed them, including the men of Shechem and all who aided in the killing of his brothers. The spirit did "bring" feelings up within the men of Shechem to rob all who passed by them along a mountainous pass. The word came to Abimelech. Meanwhile, Gaal and his brothers came over to Shechem, got drunk and began cursing Abimelech.

Zebul heard Gaal cursing and sent word to Abimelech. "Come to Shechem at night, bring people with you and wait. When the sun is rising in the morning, rush the city and kill and wound as many as you can" (verse 40). The next day, Abimelech led his people to cut trees down and burn all the people in the city and tower. That day over three thousand died. However, a certain women dropped an upper millstone on Abimelech's head and killed him instantly. This act concluded the work of the ill spirit to repay Abimelech for his wicked deeds. All the evil of the men of Shechem God returned on their own heads and on them came the curse of Jotham.

The ability of one spirit to "bring" a valenced movement of feeling within many human beings at one time reveals one aspectual ability to move the masses of human population. The amount of human spirits moved in "bringing" feelings to reveal an observed human action in a gang, mob, or community is no greater a movement than the spirit "bringing up" such feelings in one person so that God's sovereign plan is completed.

Notice the wide spread human emotion as originated from one spirit. Some men killed, some cursed, some got drunk, some rushed a city to burn it to the ground, some followed their dictator, and one dropped a millstone on Abimelech's head. The bringing up of feelings motivated many to their own death, some to not control their tongue, and many to fight vigorously.

In today's culture, we would explain such behavior in psychological terminology. For example, a murderer might be described as anti-social, narcissistic, depressive disorder with a multiaxial system classification. Moreover, the court system may require an assessment be completed to determine the nature of psychological illness. Upon a completed assessment, a treatment plan would be determined and proposed to the court.

The role of emotion in feeling has little to do with terminology for classification. In fact, the classification process, as stated in psychology, designates human behavior rather than emotional manifestation. As in Abimelech's case, his human behavior could be classified but the spirit working within his spirit had significant causal affect.

Each spirit is without partiality and hypocrisy (James 3:17). Spirits bring up feelings which moves, drives, motivates, slows, and quickens human mobility. Every emotion has recognizable feeling. Theologically, feelings are not described in clear specificity. Moreover, they are described affectively and in manifest.

For example, Scriptures state "we groan (Greek *stenazo,* meaning in straits, from *stenos,* meaning narrow) within ourselves" (Romans 8:23; 2 Corinthians 5:2). The narrow strait is always the means by which the spirit brings up feelings. It also describes the spirit has a multiplicity of choice in bringing up feelings, i.e. straits. The passage way is the same within the spirit of life, but the volume, speed, purpose, and constraint is singly the spirit's choice (Psalm 55:4; Jeremiah 4:19). Human cognition is neuropsychologically dependent upon that which the spirits sees (John 11:33; Psalm 6:6; 102:5; Judges 2:18; Ezekiel 30:24).

God said to Ezekiel (Ezekiel 37:12-14), "I will put my spirit in you and you shall live…and performed (Hebrew *asah,* meaning to do or make) it." To perform is to cause thoughts and intents within the human spirit. In Jeremiah 23:20, God performs (Hebrew *quwm,* meaning to rise) thoughts in the heart. He even performs, i.e. causes to rise, the intents of a human heart (Jeremiah 30:24). When Nabuchadnezzar was driven out of his kingdom (Daniel 4), the spirits drove him from men and into the fields to eat grass for food like the oxen. After seven years his understanding returned and he said "For His dominion is an everlasting dominion and His kingdom is from generation to generation. All the inhabitants of the earth are reputed as nothing; He does according to His will in the army of heaven and among the inhabitants of the earth. No one can restrain His hand or say to Him, 'what have you done?'"

In Job 7:11, Job said he would speak in the anguish (Hebrew *tsar,* means narrow, a tight place) of his spirit. The feelings associated with anguish, i.e. extreme pain, is theologically descriptive of the space within the spirit of life used to bring up extreme painful feelings. The entire dimensional space within the spirit of a human being is not needed to bring up an extreme level of pain. In fact, narrow in space is used.

Solomon described a merry heart makes a cheerful countenance, but by sorrow of the heart the spirit is broken (Proverbs 15:13). Sorrow (Hebrew *assebet,* meaning a pain from *asab,* meaning to carve [an image in the mind too painful to cognitively process]) originates in the spirit and is neurologically evident physically. The depressive episode whereby sadness or sorrow is experienced etiologically began by a spirit and ends when the spirit is broken (Hebrew *nake,* meaning smitten, from *naka,* meaning to drive away). Therefore, the manifested depressive episode concludes not by medication or cognitive therapies but by the absence of that spirit, i.e. the spirit has departed or left.

The emotional confidence level of kings of the Amorites and Canaanites, on the west side of the Jordan River, were high enough which made them ready to attack the children of Israel. When they heard that God had dried the river waters and the children of Israel walked over, the confidence level lowered. Scripture states their hearts melted (Hebrew *masas,* meaning to liquefy) neither was there spirit in them any more (Joshua 5:1). The spirit of confidence, was in more than one king, left all the kings which stood against Israel.

When the Queen of Sheba heard Solomon had great wisdom and wealth, she doubted the reports and came to see for herself if what she heard was true. She came to see Solomon herself with an inquisitive spirit. In 1 Kings 10:1-9, scriptures state "when the queen of Sheba heard of the fame of Solomon concerning the name of the LORD, she came to prove him with hard questions. And she came to Jerusalem with a very great train, with camels that bare spices, and very much gold, and precious stones: and when she was come to Solomon, she communed with him of all that was in her heart. And Solomon told her all her questions: there was not *any*thing hid from the king, which he told her not. And when the queen of Sheba had seen all Solomon's wisdom, and the house that he had built, And the meat of his table, and the sitting of his servants, and the attendance of his ministers, and their apparel, and his cupbearers, and his ascent by which he went up unto the house of the LORD; there was no more spirit in her. And she said to the king, It was a true report that I heard in mine own land of thy acts and of thy wisdom. Howbeit I believed not the words, until I came, and mine eyes had seen *it*: and, behold, the half was not told me: thy wisdom and prosperity exceedeth the fame which I heard. Happy *are* thy men, happy *are* these thy servants, which stand continually before thee, *and* that hear thy wisdom. Blessed be the LORD thy God, which delighted in thee, to set thee on the throne of Israel: because the LORD loved Israel for ever, therefore made He thee king, to do judgment and justice."

When the queen of Sheba had talked with Solomon, saw his wealth, his servants, and his dominion, the spirit of doubt left her. The affective nature of bringing up feelings in the Queen of Sheba moved her to wonder if these stories were true. Her inquisitive thirst to come and see motivated her to meet with Solomon. Finally, the spirit left her and she admitted her doubt and disbelief.

KEY WORDS

1. Bringing of feeling
2. Feeling etiology
3. Narrow strait
4. Spirit of confidence

KEY QUESTIONS

1. Where do feelings come from?
2. Does the spirit regulate human action?
3. What does affective valence in bringing feeling constitute?
4. By what measure do spirits determine a specific velocity of bringing to affect human experience?
5. How does a spirit move a human being with mobility?

Quick Scripture Reference Guide

Joshua 5:1 (NKJV)

[1] So it was, when all the kings of the Amorites who *were* on the west side of the Jordan, and all the kings of the Canaanites who *were* by the sea, heard that the LORD had dried up the waters of the Jordan from before the children of Israel until we had crossed over, that their heart melted; and there was no spirit in them any longer because of the children of Israel.

Judges 2:18 (NKJV)

[18] And when the LORD raised up judges for them, the LORD was with the judge and delivered them out of the hand of their enemies all the days of the judge; for the LORD was moved to pity by their groaning because of those who oppressed them and harassed them.

Judges 9:22-57 (NKJV)

[22] After Abimelech had reigned over Israel three years,

[23] God sent a spirit of ill will between Abimelech and the men of Shechem; and the men of Shechem dealt treacherously with Abimelech,

[24] that the crime *done* to the seventy sons of Jerubbaal might be settled and their blood be laid on Abimelech their brother, who killed them, and on the men of Shechem, who aided him in the killing of his brothers.

[25] And the men of Shechem set men in ambush against him on the tops of the mountains, and they robbed all who passed by them along that way; and it was told Abimelech.

[26] Now Gaal the son of Ebed came with his brothers and went over to Shechem; and the men of Shechem put their confidence in him.

[27] So they went out into the fields, and gathered *grapes* from their vineyards and trod *them*, and made merry. And they went into the house of their god, and ate and drank, and cursed Abimelech.

28 Then Gaal the son of Ebed said, "Who *is* Abimelech, and who *is* Shechem, that we should serve him? *Is he* not the son of Jerubbaal, and *is not* Zebul his officer? Serve the men of Hamor the father of Shechem; but why should we serve him?

29 If only this people were under my authority! Then I would remove Abimelech." So he said to Abimelech, "Increase your army and come out!"

30 When Zebul, the ruler of the city, heard the words of Gaal the son of Ebed, his anger was aroused.

31 And he sent messengers to Abimelech secretly, saying, "Take note! Gaal the son of Ebed and his brothers have come to Shechem; and here they are, fortifying the city against you.

32 Now therefore, get up by night, you and the people who *are* with you, and lie in wait in the field.

33 And it shall be, as soon as the sun is up in the morning, *that* you shall rise early and rush upon the city; and *when* he and the people who are with him come out against you, you may then do to them as you find opportunity."

34 So Abimelech and all the people who *were* with him rose by night, and lay in wait against Shechem in four companies.

35 When Gaal the son of Ebed went out and stood in the entrance to the city gate, Abimelech and the people who *were* with him rose from lying in wait.

36 And when Gaal saw the people, he said to Zebul, "Look, people are coming down from the tops of the mountains!" But Zebul said to him, "You see the shadows of the mountains as *if they were* men."

37 So Gaal spoke again and said, "See, people are coming down from the center of the land, and another company is coming from the Diviners' Terebinth Tree."

38 Then Zebul said to him, "Where indeed *is* your mouth now, with which you said, 'Who is Abimelech, that we should serve him?' *Are* not these the people whom you despised? Go out, if you will, and fight with them now."

39 So Gaal went out, leading the men of Shechem, and fought with Abimelech.

40 And Abimelech chased him, and he fled from him; and many fell wounded, to the *very* entrance of the gate.

41 Then Abimelech dwelt at Arumah, and Zebul drove out Gaal and his brothers, so that they would not dwell in Shechem.

42 And it came about on the next day that the people went out into the field, and they told Abimelech.

43 So he took his people, divided them into three companies, and lay in wait in the field. And he looked, and there were the people, coming out of the city; and he rose against them and attacked them.

44 Then Abimelech and the company that *was* with him rushed forward and stood at the entrance of the gate of the city; and the *other* two companies rushed upon all who *were* in the fields and killed them.

45 So Abimelech fought against the city all that day; he took the city and killed the people who *were* in it; and he demolished the city and sowed it with salt.

46 Now when all the men of the tower of Shechem had heard *that,* they entered the stronghold of the temple of the god Berith.

47 And it was told Abimelech that all the men of the tower of Shechem were gathered together.

48 Then Abimelech went up to Mount Zalmon, he and all the people who *were* with him. And Abimelech took an ax in his hand and cut down a bough from the trees, and took it and laid *it* on his shoulder; then he said to the people who were with him, "What you have seen me do, make haste *and* do as I *have done.*"

49 So each of the people likewise cut down his own bough and followed Abimelech, put *them* against the stronghold, and set the stronghold on fire above them, so that all the people of the tower of Shechem died, about a thousand men and women.

50 Then Abimelech went to Thebez, and he encamped against Thebez and took it.

51 But there was a strong tower in the city, and all the men and women–all the people of the city–fled there and shut themselves in; then they went up to the top of the tower.

52 So Abimelech came as far as the tower and fought against it; and he drew near the door of the tower to burn it with fire.

53 But a certain woman dropped an upper millstone on Abimelech's head and crushed his skull.

54 Then he called quickly to the young man, his armorbearer, and said to him, "Draw your sword and kill me, lest men say of me, 'A woman killed him.' "So his young man thrust him through, and he died.

55 And when the men of Israel saw that Abimelech was dead, they departed, every man to his place.

56 Thus God repaid the wickedness of Abimelech, which he had done to his father by killing his seventy brothers.

57 And all the evil of the men of Shechem God returned on their own heads, and on them came the curse of Jotham the son of Jerubbaal.

1 Kings 22:19-40 (NKJV)

19 Then *Micaiah* said, "Therefore hear the word of the LORD: I saw the LORD sitting on His throne, and all the host of heaven standing by, on His right hand and on His left.

20 And the LORD said, 'Who will persuade Ahab to go up, that he may fall at Ramoth Gilead?' So one spoke in this manner, and another spoke in that manner.

21 Then a spirit came forward and stood before the LORD, and said, 'I will persuade him.'

22 The LORD said to him, 'In what way?' So he said, 'I will go out and be a lying spirit in the mouth of all his prophets.' And the LORD said, 'You shall persuade *him,* and also prevail. Go out and do so.'

23 Therefore look! The LORD has put a lying spirit in the mouth of all these prophets of yours, and the LORD has declared disaster against you."

24 Now Zedekiah the son of Chenaanah went near and struck Micaiah on the cheek, and said, "Which way did the spirit from the LORD go from me to speak to you?"

25 And Micaiah said, "Indeed, you shall see on that day when you go into an inner chamber to hide!"

26 So the king of Israel said, "Take Micaiah, and return him to Amon the governor of the city and to Joash the king's son;

27 and say, 'Thus says the king: "Put this *fellow* in prison, and feed him with bread of affliction and water of affliction, until I come in peace." ' "

28 But Micaiah said, "If you ever return in peace, the LORD has not spoken by me." And he said, "Take heed, all you people!"

29 So the king of Israel and Jehoshaphat the king of Judah went up to Ramoth Gilead.

30 And the king of Israel said to Jehoshaphat, "I will disguise myself and go into battle; but you put on your robes." So the king of Israel disguised himself and went into battle.

31 Now the king of Syria had commanded the thirty-two captains of his chariots, saying, "Fight with no one small or great, but only with the king of Israel."

32 So it was, when the captains of the chariots saw Jehoshaphat, that they said, "Surely it *is* the king of Israel!" Therefore they turned aside to fight against him, and Jehoshaphat cried out.

33 And it happened, when the captains of the chariots saw that it *was* not the king of Israel, that they turned back from pursuing him.

34 Now a *certain* man drew a bow at random, and struck the king of Israel between the joints of his armor. So he said to the driver of his chariot, "Turn around and take me out of the battle, for I am wounded."

35 The battle increased that day; and the king was propped up in his chariot, facing the Syrians, and died at evening. The blood ran out from the wound onto the floor of the chariot.

36 Then, as the sun was going down, a shout went throughout the army, saying, "Every man to his city, and every man to his own country!"

[37] So the king died, and was brought to Samaria. And they buried the king in Samaria.

[38] Then *someone* washed the chariot at a pool in Samaria, and the dogs licked up his blood while the harlots bathed, according to the word of the LORD which He had spoken.

[39] Now the rest of the acts of Ahab, and all that he did, the ivory house which he built and all the cities that he built, *are* they not written in the book of the chronicles of the kings of Israel?

[40] So Ahab rested with his fathers. Then Ahaziah his son reigned in his place.

1 Chronicles 29:11 (NKJV)

[11] Yours, O LORD, *is* the greatness, The power and the glory, The victory and the majesty; For all *that is* in heaven and in earth *is Yours;* Yours *is* the kingdom, O LORD, And You are exalted as head over all.

Job 7:11 (NKJV)

[11] "Therefore I will not restrain my mouth; I will speak in the anguish of my spirit; I will complain in the bitterness of my soul.

Psalm 6:6 (NKJV)

[6] I am weary with my groaning; All night I make my bed swim; I drench my couch with my tears.

Psalm 22:8 (NKJV)

[8] "He trusted in the LORD, let Him rescue Him; Let Him deliver Him, since He delights in Him!"

Psalm 55:4 (NKJV)

[4] My heart is severely pained within me, And the terrors of death have fallen upon me.

Psalm 102:5 (NKJV)

[5] Because of the sound of my groaning My bones cling to my skin.

Psalm 115:3 (NKJV)

[3] But our God *is* in heaven; He does whatever He pleases.

Proverbs 15:13 (NKJV)

[13] A merry heart makes a cheerful countenance, But by sorrow of the heart the spirit is broken.

Jeremiah 4:19 (NKJV)

[19] O my soul, my soul! I am pained in my very heart! My heart makes a noise in me; I cannot hold my peace, Because you have heard, O my soul, The sound of the trumpet, The alarm of war.

Ezekiel 30:24 (NKJV)

[24] I will strengthen the arms of the king of Babylon and put My sword in his hand; but I will break Pharaoh's arms, and he will groan before him with the groanings of a mortally wounded *man*.

Daniel 4:35 (NKJV)

[35] All the inhabitants of the earth *are* reputed as nothing; He does according to His will in the army of heaven And *among* the inhabitants of the earth. No one can restrain His hand Or say to Him, "What have You done?"

John 11:33 (NKJV)

[33] Therefore, when Jesus saw her weeping, and the Jews who came with her weeping, He groaned in the spirit and was troubled.

Philippians 1:7-8 (NKJV)

7 just as it is right for me to think this of you all, because I have you in my heart, inasmuch as both in my chains and in the defense and confirmation of the gospel, you all are partakers with me of grace.

8 For God is my witness, how greatly I long for you all with the affection of Jesus Christ.

Romans 8:23 (NKJV)

23 Not only *that,* but we also who have the firstfruits of the Spirit, even we ourselves groan within ourselves, eagerly waiting for the adoption, the redemption of our body.

2 Corinthians 5:2 (NKJV)

2 For in this we groan, earnestly desiring to be clothed with our habitation which is from heaven,

Hebrews 2:18 (NKJV)

18 For in that He Himself has suffered, being tempted, He is able to aid those who are tempted.

Hebrews 4:15 (NKJV)

15 For we do not have a High Priest who cannot sympathize with our weaknesses, but was in all *points* tempted as *we are, yet* without sin.

James 3:17 (NKJV)

17 But the wisdom that is from above is first pure, then peaceable, gentle, willing to yield, full of mercy and good fruits, without partiality and without hypocrisy.

Chapter Ten – The Pathway of Emotion – Jealousy

SOURCE

The emotion 'jealousy' is a spirit (Numbers 5:14). It is defined by Merriam-Webster as "a jealous disposition, attitude or feeling; zealous vigilance [alertly watchful]; 1. A: intolerant of rivalry or unfaithfulness; B: disposed to suspect rivalry or unfaithfulness; 2: hostile toward a rival or one believed to enjoy an advantage; 3: vigilant in guarding a possession." To be jealous is to have zeal. Zeal is an "eagerness and ardent [characterized by warmth of feeling expressed in eager zealous support or activity] interest in pursuit of something."

Sagarin and Guadagno (2004) defined jealousy as the emotion that occurs when a person either fears losing or has already lost an important relationship with another person. While DeSteno, Valdesolo, and Barlett (2006) said jealousy was best described as a combination or blend of the feelings of anger, anxiety, betrayal, and hurt. Puente and Cohen (2003) suggested jealousy indicates a (real or imagined) threat to the relationship – a threat made especially serious when one feels a strong need for a particular person because that person cannot be replaced.

The Christian Scriptures state God is jealous (Deuteronomy 4:24, 5:9, 6:15; Joshua 24:19; Ezekiel 39:25; Nahum 1:2; Zechariah 1:14). He is a consuming fire [Hebrew *esh,* meaning fire], moreover His jealousy is consuming (Exodus 34:14; Deuteronomy 4:24). Therefore, God is consumed with eagerness and a warmth feeling in always seeing.

According to 1 Kings 22, spirits are sent to human beings. Each sent spirit is under decree from God to fulfill His demand. The means by which the spirit fulfills the decree belongs to the spirit. The spirit works within the familial, culture, work, and values in one or many until the fulfillment is accomplished.

PATHWAY

Spirits travel in the fifth dimension (White, 2007) or through the gateway (Ezekiel 40:3) [fourth dimension, white, et al.]. They appear in the same time, i.e. reality, and comes (Numbers 5:14, 30 [mind travel, i.e. what the spirit sees in its mind is reality of space and time]) upon the specified person. The spirit is seated in the persons spirit of life whereby it provokes (Hebrew *marah,* meaning to be [causal] bitter) emotion (Ezekiel 8:1-3). The spirit is free to provoke (Deuteronomy 32:16; 1 Kings 14:22) [Hebrew *Ka ac,* meaning to trouble] the human being in jealousy or move (Hebrew *qana,* meaning to be [causative make] zealous) the person toward the emotion of jealousy (Deuteronomy 32:21; Psalm 78:58).

BEHAVIOR

In Numbers 5:11-31, the law of jealousy is stated as, "if any man's wife goes astray and behaves unfaithfully toward him and a man lies with her carnally, and it is hidden from the eyes of her husband, and it is concealed that she has defiled herself, and there was no witness against her, nor was she caught, if the spirit of jealousy comes upon him and he becomes jealous of his wife, who has defiled herself; or if the spirit of jealousy comes upon him and he becomes jealous of his wife, although she has not defiled herself." Either she is free and may conceive children or the man shall be free from iniquity but the woman shall bear her guilt.

In Psalm 78:58, the people moved him, meaning to waver in mind, will, feeling irresolutely between choices, (Hebrew *qana,* meaning to be [causative make] zealous; to jealousy with their carved images. The people provoked (Hebrew *Ka as*, meaning to trouble) God to anger.

In Proverbs 6:34-35 Jealousy is a rage (Hebrew *hema,* meaning heat, from *yaham,* meaning to be hot) manifested by spirit in God (Deuteronomy 4:24; Joshua 24:19) or in man. The movement of the spirit of jealousy in man moved him by the heat of the spirit. The heat of the spirit in man may intensify his level of anger to become furious. The intensity of heat is causal and affective in man's behavior ranging from calm to furious. Such fury of anger could move a person to vengeance not accepting appeasement.

Pfeiffer and Wong (1989) posited cognitive and behavioral jealousy become pathological to the extent that they cause obsessive or anxiety disorders and interfere with the individual's daily functioning. To be pathological refers to the study of mental disorders – their problems, causes, and process involving impairments, deviance, and distress, producing clinically significant impairment or distress in one's personal, social, or occupational life (Maxmen, Ward, 1995).

The spirit of jealousy manifests itself in human behavior. Some research suggests jealousy related emotions are observable. Guerrero, Trost, and Yoshimura (2005) sighted six basic composites of jealousy-related emotion from White and Mullen (1989). The anger cluster included hate, contempt, and annoyance; the fear cluster included anxiety, tension, worry, and distress; the sadness cluster included depression and hopelessness; the envy cluster included envy, resentment, and covetousness; sexual arousal cluster includes sexual arousal, lust, and passion; and a guilt cluster included guilt, regret, and embarrassment.

Jealousy is also one direction not just in relationship between people. God is jealous for his land [Israel] (Joel 2:18; Zechariah 1:14, 8:2). God loves Israel and keeps His eye on her. God's jealousy causes vengeful repayment for those who hurt Israel, and on His adversaries (Nahum 1:2). It is the spirit of jealousy that moves or provokes God to be vengeful. He is not vengeful while looking for people to be mean to or retaliate bad upon.

CONCLUSION

The emotion jealousy is a spirit. It has been defined as an observable behavior and from the Christian Scriptures. The etiological framework of how the emotion begins and is characterized has been established as a spirit. The behavior exhibited by people, between people, and for people manifests itself either in fears of losing, or having already lost an important relationship. And it can be one-directional toward a nation.

KEY WORDS

1. Fifth dimension
2. Jealousy

KEY QUESTIONS

1. Define jealousy.
2. Where does the spirit sit before "seeing" reality?
3. How does the spirit of jealousy move a human being?

Quick Scripture Reference Guide

Exodus 34:14 (NKJV)

14 (for you shall worship no other god, for the LORD, whose name *is* Jealous, *is* a jealous God),

Numbers 5:14 (NKJV)

14 if the spirit of jealousy comes upon him and he becomes jealous of his wife, who has defiled herself; or if the spirit of jealousy comes upon him and he becomes jealous of his wife, although she has not defiled herself–

Numbers 5:30 (NKJV)

30 or when the spirit of jealousy comes upon a man, and he becomes jealous of his wife; then he shall stand the woman before the LORD, and the priest shall execute all this law upon her.

Deuteronomy 4:24 (NKJV)

24 For the LORD your God *is* a consuming fire, a jealous God.

Deuteronomy 5:9 (NKJV)

9 you shall not bow down to them nor serve them. For I, the LORD your God, *am* a jealous God, visiting the iniquity of the fathers upon the children to the third and fourth *generations* of those who hate Me,

Deuteronomy 6:15 (NKJV)

15 (for the LORD your God *is* a jealous God among you), lest the anger of the LORD your God be aroused against you and destroy you from the face of the earth.

Deuteronomy 32:16 (NKJV)

16 They provoked Him to jealousy with foreign *gods;* With abominations they provoked Him to anger.

Deuteronomy 32:21 (NKJV)

21 They have provoked Me to jealousy by *what* is not God; They have moved Me to anger by their foolish idols. But I will provoke them to jealousy by *those who are* not a nation; I will move them to anger by a foolish nation.

Joshua 24:19 (NKJV)

19 But Joshua said to the people, "You cannot serve the LORD, for He *is* a holy God. He *is* a jealous God; He will not forgive your transgressions nor your sins.

1 Kings 14:22 (NKJV)

22 Now Judah did evil in the sight of the LORD, and they provoked Him to jealousy with their sins which they committed, more than all that their fathers had done.

Psalm 78:58 (NKJV)

58 For they provoked Him to anger with their high places, And moved Him to jealousy with their carved images.

Proverbs 6:34-35 (NKJV)

34 For jealousy *is* a husband's fury; Therefore he will not spare in the day of vengeance.

35 He will accept no recompense, Nor will he be appeased though you give many gifts.

Ezekiel 8:1-3 (NKJV)

1 And it came to pass in the sixth year, in the sixth *month,* on the fifth *day* of the month, as I sat in my house with the elders of Judah sitting before me, that the hand of the Lord GOD fell upon me there.

2 Then I looked, and there was a likeness, like the appearance of fire–from the appearance of His waist and downward, fire; and from His waist and upward, like the appearance of brightness, like the color of amber.

[3] He stretched out the form of a hand, and took me by a lock of my hair; and the Spirit lifted me up between earth and heaven, and brought me in visions of God to Jerusalem, to the door of the north gate of the inner *court,* where the seat of the image of jealousy *was,* which provokes to jealousy.

Ezekiel 39:25 (NKJV)

[25] "Therefore thus says the Lord GOD: 'Now I will bring back the captives of Jacob, and have mercy on the whole house of Israel; and I will be jealous for My holy name–

Ezekiel 40:3 (NKJV)

[3] He took me there, and behold, *there was* a man whose appearance *was* like the appearance of bronze. He had a line of flax and a measuring rod in his hand, and he stood in the gateway.

Joel 2:18 (NKJV)

[18] Then the LORD will be zealous for His land, And pity His people.

Nahum 1:2 (NKJV)

[2] God *is* jealous, and the LORD avenges; The LORD avenges and *is* furious. The LORD will take vengeance on His adversaries, And He reserves *wrath* for His enemies;

Zechariah 1:14 (NKJV)

[14] So the angel who spoke with me said to me, "Proclaim, saying, 'Thus says the LORD of hosts: "I am zealous for Jerusalem And for Zion with great zeal.

Zechariah 8:2 (NKJV)

[2] "Thus says the LORD of hosts: 'I am zealous for Zion with great zeal; With great fervor I am zealous for her.'

Chapter Eleven – The Pathway of Emotion – Heaviness

SOURCE

In Isaiah 61:3, the prophet describes responsibilities of the Messiah. One of His duties while on earth is to give the garment of praise for the spirit of heaviness (Hebrew *Keheh,* meaning feeble from *kaha,* meaning to be weak) or a glad heart inclined to praise God in lieu of a heavy heart in despair (Spence, Exell). This spirit is universal to everyone.

The spirit of heaviness causes a human being to be emotionally sick i.e. depressed (Psalm 69:20). In Proverbs 12:25 this spirit makes the heart stoop (Hebrew *shaha,* meaning to depress). In the NKJV – "anxiety in the heart of man causes depression". Heaviness of spirit prevents kindness of spirit from "seeing" (Nehemiah 9:17; Psalm 21:21; Joel 2:13; Acts 28:2). When the spirit of heaviness "sees", you are unable to be kind.

PATHWAY

Spirits travel in the fifth dimension (White, 2007) or through the gateway (Ezekiel 40:3) [fourth dimension, White, et al.]. They appear in the same time i.e. reality, and comes (Numbers 5:14, 30 [mind travel, i.e. what the spirit sees in its mind is reality of space and time]) upon the specified person. The spirit is seated in the persons' spirit of life whereby it provokes (Hebrew *marah*, meaning to be [causal] bitter) emotion (Ezekiel 8:1-3). The spirit is free to provoke (Deuteronomy 32:16; 1 Kings 14:22).

BEHAVIOR

The affective nature of this spirit within the heart of a human being is etiological in causation of mood change. Such change is reflected in emotional feelings: abandonment, annoyed, anxious, bewildered, gored, defeated, defensive, depressed, detached, disappointed, disgusted, distant, distrustful, disturbed, edgy, empty, fearful, frustrated, furious, grief, glum, helpless, hollow, humiliated, hurt, inadequate, intense, intimidated, irritable, isolated, lonely, loss, miserable, neglected, pessimistic, pressured, put down, puzzled, rejected, sad, separated, shame, subdued, tired, uneasy, upset, uptight, used, void, vulnerable, weak, and worried.

In the Beck Depression Inventory, feelings are characterized by twenty-one areas of feelings: sadness, pessimism, past failure, loss of pleasure, guilty feelings, punishment feelings, self-dislike, self-criticalness, suicidal thoughts or wishes, crying, agitation, loss of interest, indecisiveness, worthlessness, loss of energy, changes in sleeping pattern, irritability, changes in appetite, concentration difficulty, tiredness or fatigue, and loss of interest in sex. It is possible that clinical scales of Hypochondriasis, Depression, Psychopathic Deviant, Paranoia, Psychasthenia and Social Introversion (Groth-Marnat, 2003); Maxmen, Ward, 1995) may be distressed properties which could reveal causal pathology from the spirit of heaviness.

In Psalm 69:20, David's heart was broken (Hebrew *shabar,* meaning to burst) and he was full of heaviness. He also used the Hebrew word *dalap,* meaning to drip, describing his melting heart of depression (Psalm 119:28). The affective release is determined by the spirit of heaviness. This spirit could release "seeing" in degrees of melt (Psalm 119:28, Hebrew *dalaph,* to drip), great (Romans 9:2, Greek *megas,* big), or full (Psalm 69:20; Philippians 2:26, Greek *Kor-en-noo-mee,* to cram, i.e. glut or sate).

In Ezra 9:1-5 leaders came to Ezra and told him "the people of Israel and the priests and the Levites have not separated themselves from the peoples of the lands...for they have taken some of their daughters as wives for themselves and their sons, so that the holy seed is mixed with the peoples of the lands...so

(Ezra) tore his garment, and robe, plucked out some of the hair of his head and beard. "At evening sacrifice he arose from his heaviness" (Hebrew *ta anit,* meaning affliction, from *ana,* meaning to depress). The spirit of heaviness saw what some in Israel had done and depressed Ezra. The heaviness was so great he felt emotionally afflicted. The spirit of heaviness determined the level of affliction. Ezra could not regulate the emotional level of depression. Regulation of emotion is spirit determined.

In Proverbs 16:19 and 29:23 Solomon states there is a humble spirit. Moreover, the prophet Isaiah states this spirit is from God. I believe the spirit of heaviness can also "see" humility. Isaiah describes that God has a contrite (Hebrew *dakka,* meaning crushed from *dakah,* meaning to crumble) and humble (Hebrew *shapal,* meaning depressed from *shapel,* meaning to depress or sink) spirit. Two examples of this affect of spirit are described by David (Psalm 38:18, 51:17, 147:3 and Isaiah 66:2).

Isaiah 57:15 (NKJV), "for thus says the high and lofty One who inhabits eternity, whose name is Holy: I dwell in the high and holy place, with him who has a contrite and humble spirit, to revive the spirit of the humble and to revive the heart of the contrite ones." This spirit is in every human being and may be revived (Hebrew *haya,* meaning to live). When this spirit enters the spirit of life within a human being it causes depression.

The American Psychiatric Association describes a depressive episode as featuring a depressed mood or the loss of interest, or pleasure in nearly all activities. Symptoms present during the same two – week period and represent a change from previous functioning which do not include symptoms due to a general medical condition include: 1) depressed mood most of the day; 2) markedly diminished interest or pleasure in all or almost all activities most of the day; 3) significant weight loss when not dieting or weight gain; 4) insomnia or hypersomnia nearly every day; 5) psychomotor agitation; 6) fatigue or loss of energy nearly every day; 7) feelings of worthlessness or excessive or inappropriate guilt; 8) diminished ability to think or concentrate or indecisiveness nearly every day; 9) recurrent thoughts of death (DSM-IV).

Webster describes humble as not proud or haughty; not arrogant or assertive; reflecting, expressing, or offering in a spirit of deference or submission. Wilson (Word Studies) defined humble to be low in situation, in mind, in condition, or any other respect. Unfortunately Wilson did not define "low" in his definition.

Hastings sighted humility as a union of highest self-respect with uttermost abandon of sacrifice in service. "A man who knows his own superior worth and yet is willing to serve his inferiors is a human man". He further states "genuine humility loses all its self-conceit but never loses its self-respect".

CONCLUSION

The emotion of heaviness is a spirit. As stated earlier it is defined as (Hebrew *keheh*, meaning feeble from *kaha*, meaning to be weak) a glad heart inclined to praise God in lieu of a heavy heart in despair (Spence, Exell). The spirit of heaviness causes a human being to be emotionally sick i.e. distressed (Psalm 69:20). The etiological framework of how the emotion begins and is characterized has been established as spirit. The behavior exhibited by people, between people and for people manifests itself as a depressed mood. The crushing affect of this spirit has many options available by which the effect of behavior is manifested.

KEY WORDS

1. Spirit of heaviness
2. Mood change

KEY QUESTIONS

1. Explain the pathway of emotional heaviness?
2. Define the meaning of heaviness?
3. What affect does this spirit have on human beings?
4. Does this spirit cause depression?

Quick Scripture Reference Guide

Deuteronomy 32:16 (NKJV)

[16] They provoked Him to jealousy with foreign *gods;* With abominations they provoked Him to anger.

1 Kings 14:22 (NKJV)

[22] Now Judah did evil in the sight of the LORD, and they provoked Him to jealousy with their sins which they committed, more than all that their fathers had done.

Ezra 9:1-5 (NKJV)

[1] When these things were done, the leaders came to me, saying, "The people of Israel and the priests and the Levites have not separated themselves from the peoples of the lands, with respect to the abominations of the Canaanites, the Hittites, the Perizzites, the Jebusites, the Ammonites, the Moabites, the Egyptians, and the Amorites.

[2] For they have taken some of their daughters *as wives* for themselves and their sons, so that the holy seed is mixed with the peoples of *those* lands. Indeed, the hand of the leaders and rulers has been foremost in this trespass."

[3] So when I heard this thing, I tore my garment and my robe, and plucked out some of the hair of my head and beard, and sat down astonished.

[4] Then everyone who trembled at the words of the God of Israel assembled to me, because of the transgression of those who had been carried away captive, and I sat astonished until the evening sacrifice.

[5] At the evening sacrifice I arose from my fasting; and having torn my garment and my robe, I fell on my knees and spread out my hands to the LORD my God.

Nehemiah 9:17 (NKJV)

[17] They refused to obey, And they were not mindful of Your wonders That You did among them. But they hardened their necks, And in their rebellion They appointed a leader To return to their bondage. But You *are* God, Ready to pardon, Gracious and merciful, Slow to anger, Abundant in kindness, And did not forsake them.

Psalm 31:21 (NKJV)

[21] Blessed *be* the LORD, For He has shown me His marvelous kindness in a strong city!

Psalm 38:18 (NKJV)

[18] For I will declare my iniquity; I will be in anguish over my sin.

Psalm 51:17 (NKJV)

[17] The sacrifices of God *are* a broken spirit, A broken and a contrite heart– These, O God, You will not despise.

Psalm 69:20 (NKJV)

[20] Reproach has broken my heart, And I am full of heaviness; I looked *for someone* to take pity, but *there was* none; And for comforters, but I found none.

Psalm 119:28 (NKJV)

[28] My soul melts from heaviness; Strengthen me according to Your word.

Psalm 147:3 (NKJV)

[3] He heals the brokenhearted And binds up their wounds.

Proverbs 12:25 (NKJV)

[25] Anxiety in the heart of man causes depression, But a good word makes it glad.

Proverbs 16:19 (NKJV)

19 Better *to be* of a humble spirit with the lowly, Than to divide the spoil with the proud.

Proverbs 29:23 (NKJV)

23 A man's pride will bring him low, But the humble in spirit will retain honor.

Isaiah 57:15 (NKJV)

15 For thus says the High and Lofty One Who inhabits eternity, whose name *is* Holy: "I dwell in the high and holy *place,* With him *who* has a contrite and humble spirit, To revive the spirit of the humble, And to revive the heart of the contrite ones.

Isaiah 61:3 (NKJV)

3 To console those who mourn in Zion, To give them beauty for ashes, The oil of joy for mourning, The garment of praise for the spirit of heaviness; That they may be called trees of righteousness, The planting of the LORD, that He may be glorified."

Isaiah 66:2 (NKJV)

2 For all those *things* My hand has made, And all those *things* exist," Says the LORD. "But on this *one* will I look: On *him who is* poor and of a contrite spirit, And who trembles at My word.

Ezekiel 8:1-3 (NKJV)

1 And it came to pass in the sixth year, in the sixth *month,* on the fifth *day* of the month, as I sat in my house with the elders of Judah sitting before me, that the hand of the Lord GOD fell upon me there.

2 Then I looked, and there was a likeness, like the appearance of fire–from the appearance of His waist and downward, fire; and from His waist and upward, like the appearance of brightness, like the color of amber.

3 He stretched out the form of a hand, and took me by a lock of my hair; and the Spirit lifted me up between earth and heaven, and brought me in visions of God

to Jerusalem, to the door of the north gate of the inner *court,* where the seat of the image of jealousy *was,* which provokes to jealousy.

Ezekiel 40:3 (NKJV)

3 He took me there, and behold, *there was* a man whose appearance *was* like the appearance of bronze. He had a line of flax and a measuring rod in his hand, and he stood in the gateway.

Joel 2:13 (NKJV)

13 So rend your heart, and not your garments; Return to the LORD your God, For He *is* gracious and merciful, Slow to anger, and of great kindness; And He relents from doing harm.

Acts 28:2 (NKJV)

2 And the natives showed us unusual kindness; for they kindled a fire and made us all welcome, because of the rain that was falling and because of the cold.

Romans 9:2 (NKJV)

2 that I have great sorrow and continual grief in my heart.

Philippians 2:26 (NKJV)

26 since he was longing for you all, and was distressed because you had heard that he was sick.

Chapter Twelve – The Pathway of Emotion – Sorrow

SOURCE

In 1 Samuel 1:15, Hannah said "I am a woman of a sorrowful (Hebrew *qasheh,* meaning severe, from *qasha,* meaning to be dense, i.e. compacted or crowded) spirit". God said to Moses, He appoints, consumes the eyes, and causes sorrow of heart (Leviticus 26:16). When He appoints (Hebrew *paqad,* meaning visit) spirits to come into the human heart, He directs them to do so (Job 21:17). When He consumes (Hebrew *kala,* meaning to end) the eyes He ends the ability of additional spirits in the spirit of life in the human being to be affective. Then He causes (Hebrew *dub,* meaning to mope, i.e. to act in a dazed manner; Proverbs 10:10) sorrow of heart.

PATHWAY

Spirits travel in the fifth dimension (White, 2007) or through the gateway (Ezekiel 40:3) [fourth dimension, White, et al.]. They appear in the same time i.e. reality, and comes (Numbers 5:14, 30 [mind travel, i.e. what the spirit sees in its mind is reality of space and time]) upon the specified person. The spirit is seated in the persons' spirit of life whereby it provokes (Hebrew *marah,* meaning to be [causal] bitter) emotion (Ezekiel 8:1-3). The spirit is free to provoke (Deuteronomy 32:16; 1 Kings 14:22) [Hebrew *ka ac,* meaning to trouble] the human being in the spirit of sorrow.

BEHAVIOR

In Deuteronomy 28:65, "The Lord shall give you a trembling (Hebrew *raggaz,* meaning timid) heart, a failing (Hebrew *killayon,* meaning pining, i.e. languish, to be in a state of depression or decreasing vitality) of eyes, and a sorrow (Hebrew *de' abon,* meaning pining, i.e. to languish, to be in a state of depression or decreasing vitality) of mind." According to the Scriptures, God sends spirits into the spirit of life in a human being failing what the spirit "sees" in order to afford the human being an experience of grief or emotion appealing to sympathy or empathy (Jeremiah 45:3; Lamentations 3:32). Sympathy is defined as feeling sorry for someone. Empathy is an understanding of the feelings and concerns of others (Berger, 2008).

A grieving (Hebrew *sheber,* meaning to fracture, from *shabar,* meaning to burst) spirit (Isaiah 65:14) is emotionally heavy (Hebrew *kabed,* Job 6:2-4). Job called grief a poison (Hebrew *hema,* meaning heat). When the spirit of grief "sees", it consumes (Hebrew *ashash,* meaning to shrink, i.e. emotional groaning, affecting physical strength and overall body strength) the eyes (Psalm 6:7; 31:9). The shrinking intensifies the emotional level causing distress and affectual heaviness of spirit.

The spirit of grief sits in the spirit of life to "see" (Genesis 6:6; Deuteronomy 15:10; 1 Samuel 1:8, 2:23; Psalm 73:21). Jesus said grief hardens (Greek *porosis,* meaning to behave with stupidity from *poroo,* meaning to petrify, i.e. harden as stoned) the heart (Mark 3:5). The affect of this spirit has behavioral and emotional change in the human being.

The spirit of grief is not bound by the dimension of time but remains within the spirit of life until its purpose has been completed. Some spirits remain within for forty years (Psalm 95:10; Hebrews 3:17), while others have this spirit their entire life (psalm 31:10; Isaiah 15:4). These two examples are not standards of inhabituation.

The sorrow of heart (Nehemiah 2:2; Proverbs 15:13; Isaiah 65:14) may be stirred (Hebrew *akar,* meaning to roil, i.e. to stir up: disturb, disorder: to move turbulently: be in a state of turbulence or agitation, i.e. conflicting emotion~inside her) up (Psalm 39:2-3) or added to (Jeremiah 45:3). This spirit could release "seeing" in degrees of sorrowful (Mark 14:19) as very (Hebrew *me' od,* meaning vehemence i.e. intensely emotional) (Zechariah 9:5; Luke 18:23-24), and exceeding (Greek *sphodra,* meaning violent) (Matthew 26:22, 38; Mark 14:34).

Eakes and Burke (1999) sighted Lindgren, Burke, Hainsworth, and Eakes (1992) which provided an analyses on the concept of sorrow to clarify the nature of chronic sorrow and articulated the following defining characteristics:

1. A perception of sadness or sorrow over time in a situation with no predictable end.
2. Sadness or sorrow that is cyclic or recurrent.
3. Sadness or sorrow that is triggered internally or externally and brings to mind the person's losses, disappointments, or fear.
4. Sadness or sorrow that is progressive and can intensify.

From this research, sorrow has a triggered mechanism which predisposes sadness or sorrow on the human being. However, Scripture does not support a triggering episode or event. Specifically, the spirit "sees" and the human being experiences sadness or sorrow. Proverbs 15:13 states the spirit is broken (Hebrew *shabar,* meaning to burst; Psalms 109:16, 147:3; Proverbs 15:13, 17:22; Ezekiel 6:9) to experience sorrow of the heart.

Ahlstrom (2007) found chronic sorrow was affective to repeated loss. He sighted loss from people who have a progressive disease whereby they gradually, on repeated occasions, have lowered bodily capacities, the principle loss being the ability to move from one of these: 1) they cannot live the life they lived before or the life they had imagined living; 2) the loss of the ability to move about freely; 3) the inability to participate in daily life; 4) loss of identity; 5) loss of uplifting emotions; 6) loss of relish for life; 7) loss of relationships; and 8) loss of integrity and privacy.

CONCLUSION

God appoints and directs spirits to consume the eyes and cause sorrow of heart. The spirit is free to provoke the human being in the spirit of sorrow. The affect of this spirit has behavioral and emotional regulatory possession as valenced in each spirit of life.

KEY WORDS

1. Sorrowful spirit
2. Spirit of grief

KEY QUESTIONS

1. Explain how sorrow of heart mirrors depression?
2. What do you believe about God sending spirits into human beings in order that they become depressed?
3. How does the spirit cause sorrow?
4. How involved is God in the everyday emotions of human beings?

Quick Scripture Reference Guide

Genesis 6:6 (NKJV)

6 And the LORD was sorry that He had made man on the earth, and He was grieved in His heart.

Leviticus 26:16 (NKJV)

16 I also will do this to you: I will even appoint terror over you, wasting disease and fever which shall consume the eyes and cause sorrow of heart. And you shall sow your seed in vain, for your enemies shall eat it.

Numbers 5:13-14 (NKJV)

13 and a man lies with her carnally, and it is hidden from the eyes of her husband, and it is concealed that she has defiled herself, and *there was* no witness against her, nor was she caught–

14 if the spirit of jealousy comes upon him and he becomes jealous of his wife, who has defiled herself; or if the spirit of jealousy comes upon him and he becomes jealous of his wife, although she has not defiled herself–

Deuteronomy 15:10 (NKJV)

10 You shall surely give to him, and your heart should not be grieved when you give to him, because for this thing the LORD your God will bless you in all your works and in all to which you put your hand.

Deuteronomy 28:65 (NKJV)

65 And among those nations you shall find no rest, nor shall the sole of your foot have a resting place; but there the LORD will give you a trembling heart, failing eyes, and anguish of soul.

Deuteronomy 32:16 (NKJV)

[16] They provoked Him to jealousy with foreign *gods;* With abominations they provoked Him to anger.

1 Samuel 1:8 (NKJV)

[8] Then Elkanah her husband said to her, "Hannah, why do you weep? Why do you not eat? And why is your heart grieved? *Am* I not better to you than ten sons?"

1 Samuel 1:15 (NKJV)

[15] And Hannah answered and said, "No, my lord, I *am* a woman of sorrowful spirit. I have drunk neither wine nor intoxicating drink, but have poured out my soul before the LORD.

1 Samuel 2:23 (NKJV)

[23] So he said to them, "Why do you do such things? For I hear of your evil dealings from all the people.

1 Kings 14:22 (NKJV)

[22] Now Judah did evil in the sight of the LORD, and they provoked Him to jealousy with their sins which they committed, more than all that their fathers had done.

Nehemiah 2:2 (NKJV)

[2] Therefore the king said to me, "Why *is* your face sad, since you *are* not sick? This *is* nothing but sorrow of heart." So I became dreadfully afraid,

Job 6:2-4 (NKJV)

[2] "Oh, that my grief were fully weighed, And my calamity laid with it on the scales!

[3] For then it would be heavier than the sand of the sea– Therefore my words have been rash.

[4] For the arrows of the Almighty *are* within me; My spirit drinks in their poison; The terrors of God are arrayed against me.

Job 21:17 (NKJV)

17 "How often is the lamp of the wicked put out? *How often* does their destruction come upon them, The sorrows *God* distributes in His anger?

Psalm 6:7 (NKJV)

7 My eye wastes away because of grief; It grows old because of all my enemies.

Psalm 31:9 (NKJV)

9 Have mercy on me, O LORD, for I am in trouble; My eye wastes away with grief, *Yes,* my soul and my body!

Psalm 31:10 (NKJV)

10 For my life is spent with grief, And my years with sighing; My strength fails because of my iniquity, And my bones waste away.

Psalm 39:2-3 (NKJV)

2 I was mute with silence, I held my peace *even* from good; And my sorrow was stirred up.

3 My heart was hot within me; While I was musing, the fire burned. *Then* I spoke with my tongue:

Psalm 73:21 (NKJV)

21 Thus my heart was grieved, And I was vexed in my mind.

Psalm 95:10 (NKJV)

10 For forty years I was grieved with *that* generation, And said, 'It *is* a people who go astray in their hearts, And they do not know My ways.'

Psalm 109:16 (NKJV)

16 Because he did not remember to show mercy, But persecuted the poor and needy man, That he might even slay the broken in heart.

Psalm 147:3 (NKJV)

3 He heals the brokenhearted And binds up their wounds.

Proverbs 10:10 (NKJV)

10 He who winks with the eye causes trouble, But a prating fool will fall.

Proverbs 15:13 (NKJV)

13 A merry heart makes a cheerful countenance, But by sorrow of the heart the spirit is broken.

Proverbs 17:22 (NKJV)

22 A merry heart does good, *like* medicine, But a broken spirit dries the bones.

Isaiah 15:4 (NKJV)

4 Heshbon and Elealeh will cry out, Their voice shall be heard as far as Jahaz; Therefore the armed soldiers of Moab will cry out; His life will be burdensome to him.

Isaiah 65:14 (NKJV)

14 Behold, My servants shall sing for joy of heart, But you shall cry for sorrow of heart, And wail for grief of spirit.

Jeremiah 45:3 (NKJV)

3 'You said, "Woe is me now! For the LORD has added grief to my sorrow. I fainted in my sighing, and I find no rest." '

Lamentations 3:32 (NKJV)

32 Though He causes grief, Yet He will show compassion According to the multitude of His mercies.

Ezekiel 8:1-3 (NKJV)

1 And it came to pass in the sixth year, in the sixth *month,* on the fifth *day* of the month, as I sat in my house with the elders of Judah sitting before me, that the hand of the Lord GOD fell upon me there.

2 Then I looked, and there was a likeness, like the appearance of fire–from the appearance of His waist and downward, fire; and from His waist and upward, like the appearance of brightness, like the color of amber.

3 He stretched out the form of a hand, and took me by a lock of my hair; and the Spirit lifted me up between earth and heaven, and brought me in visions of God to Jerusalem, to the door of the north gate of the inner *court,* where the seat of the image of jealousy *was,* which provokes to jealousy.

Ezekiel 6:9 (NKJV)

9 Then those of you who escape will remember Me among the nations where they are carried captive, because I was crushed by their adulterous heart which has departed from Me, and by their eyes which play the harlot after their idols; they will loathe themselves for the evils which they committed in all their abominations.

Ezekiel 40:3 (NKJV)

3 He took me there, and behold, *there was* a man whose appearance *was* like the appearance of bronze. He had a line of flax and a measuring rod in his hand, and he stood in the gateway.

Zechariah 9:5 (NKJV)

5 Ashkelon shall see *it* and fear; Gaza also shall be very sorrowful; And Ekron, for He dried up her expectation. The king shall perish from Gaza, And Ashkelon shall not be inhabited.

Matthew 26:22 (NKJV)

22 And they were exceedingly sorrowful, and each of them began to say to Him, "Lord, is it I?"

Matthew 26:38 (NKJV)

38 Then He said to them, "My soul is exceedingly sorrowful, even to death. Stay here and watch with Me."

Mark 3:5 (NKJV)

5 And when He had looked around at them with anger, being grieved by the hardness of their hearts, He said to the man, "Stretch out your hand." And he stretched *it* out, and his hand was restored as whole as the other.

Mark 14:19 (NKJV)

19 And they began to be sorrowful, and to say to Him one by one, "*Is* it I?" And another *said*, "*Is* it I?"

Mark 14:34 (NKJV)

34 Then He said to them, "My soul is exceedingly sorrowful, *even* to death. Stay here and watch."

Luke 18:22-24 (NKJV)

22 So when Jesus heard these things, He said to him, "You still lack one thing. Sell all that you have and distribute to the poor, and you will have treasure in heaven; and come, follow Me."

23 But when he heard this, he became very sorrowful, for he was very rich.

24 And when Jesus saw that he became very sorrowful, He said, "How hard it is for those who have riches to enter the kingdom of God!

Hebrews 3:17 (NKJV)

17 Now with whom was He angry forty years? *Was it* not with those who sinned, whose corpses fell in the wilderness?

Chapter Thirteen – Emotion Identity

BERGER (2008) OUTLINES A PROGRESSIVE formative research based hypothesis on emotional development throughout the lifespan. In this chapter a cumulative gathering of data from Berger describes observable emotional behavior. She stated, "Beginning at birth emotions emerge with a variety of expression (e.g. crying, social smile, laughter, responsive smiles, anger, fear, and self awareness) during the first eighteen months. New emotions emerge which require an awareness of other people through family interactions.

Through experience, social interactions develop. A new sense of self or self awareness emerges into self recognition. From ages 2 to 6, children master emotional regulation which is defined as the ability to control when and how emotions are expressed. When a child cannot control emotion impulse, developmentalists suggests the first signs of psychopathology in children usually involve emotions that seem to overwhelm the child.

A child's ability to regulate emotions requires thinking before acting. Therefore, emotional regulation is the province of the prefrontal cortex, the executive area of the brain. Berger further explained emotions need regulation not repression, since over control, not just under control, can lead to psychological problems.

Children ages, 6 to 11, have an ability to understand social cognition which is the ability to understand human interactions and improve in their ability, called effortful control, which entails modifying impulses and emotions. With this ability children formulate a self-concept, including social comparison, effortful control, loyalty, and appreciation of peers and parents, to increase their self understanding.

Adolescent egocentrism is evident at the beginning of adolescence. Emotionally, adolescents try to make sense of conflicting feelings about their own parents, school, and classmates. Egocentric means "self at the center", which may signal growth toward cognitive maturity. Adolescents find it much easier and quicker to forget about logic and follow their impulses.

Identity is defined as a consistent definition of one's self as a unique individual, in terms of roles, attitudes, beliefs and aspirations. At this stage of development the person tries to figure out "Who am I?" This is accomplished while adolescents seek to establish their own identities by reconsidering all the goals and values set by their parents and culture, accepting some and rejecting others.

Erickson highlighted four aspects of identity: religion, sex, politics (i.e. Republican, Independent, or Democrat) and vocation. Sexual identity, or gender identity, refers to a person's self-definition as a male or female. During adolescents, combing and consolidating emotions and logic is a crucial intellectual accomplishment.

Emerging adults age, 18 to 25, are still seeking to establish who they are. They have more partners and more sexual intercourse. Their attitudes about sex are likely to produce emotional stress, labeled as an unanticipated emotional entanglement. Both positive and negative emotions seem to be especially strong at this time.

During late adulthood, identity requires a reassessment. Identity is challenged in old age. The usual pillars of the self-concept crumble, specifically appearance, health, and employment. During this stage in their life, a person combines long-standing identity with changing circumstances, avoiding both resistance (assimilation) and total defeat (accommodation)."

As Berger noted, the means by which identity is identified changes throughout the life span. Beginning with emotion identification and progression through external identifiers, researchers have gathered empirical data supporting their findings.

However, theologically, self is identified by the spirit. When God, who is a spirit, identified himself to Isaac, he said "I am the God of your father Abraham" (Genesis 26:24, 28:13). To Jacob, He said, "I am God Almighty" (Genesis 35:11). When Moses came before God at the burning bush, God identified Himself as "I am who I am" (Exodus 3:14).

"I AM" (Hebrew *hayah,* meaning to exist from *hava,* meaning to breathe) identified Himself. His identity is spirit reality. The true essence of Himself is not including any psychosocial stages as Erikson described. God does not have role diffusion, isolation issues, stagnation from lack of creativity, or despair.

Emotion identity acknowledges the spirits within the spirit of life in each human being. Subject to those spirits, human beings define their identity by culture, ethnicity, vocation, family, cognition, education, intelligence, gender, socioeconomic status, disability, senescense, and personality. The essence of emotion identity is not accumulative by experience but in the here and now identifying self from the spirit of life (peaceable, gentle, willing to yield, full of mercy and good fruits, without partiality and without hypocrisy) James 3:17.

Further research on this subject should include identifying all the spirits. Determining how spirits "see" for personality development and cognition may build upon this Theological Handbook of Emotion. Emotion Identity may further be explained in research seeking to discover what spirits are involved at the moment of "seeing" and does human age have limitations of spirit expression.

KEY WORDS

1. Emotion identity
2. Identity
3. Self

KEY QUESTIONS

1. How do human beings define themselves today?
2. How has psychology changed the way we describe ourselves?
3. What is the essence of spirit identity?

Quick Scripture Reference Guide

Genesis 26:24 (NKJV)

24 And the LORD appeared to him the same night and said, "I *am* the God of your father Abraham; do not fear, for I *am* with you. I will bless you and multiply your descendants for My servant Abraham's sake."

Genesis 28:13 (NKJV)

13 And behold, the LORD stood above it and said: "I *am* the LORD God of Abraham your father and the God of Isaac; the land on which you lie I will give to you and your descendants.

Genesis 35:11 (NKJV)

11 Also God said to him: "I *am* God Almighty. Be fruitful and multiply; a nation and a company of nations shall proceed from you, and kings shall come from your body.

Exodus 3:14 (NKJV)

14 And God said to Moses, "I AM WHO I AM." And He said, "Thus you shall say to the children of Israel, 'I AM has sent me to you.' "

James 3:17 (NKJV)

17 But the wisdom that is from above is first pure, then peaceable, gentle, willing to yield, full of mercy and good fruits, without partiality and without hypocrisy.

Chapter Fourteen – The Pathway of Anger

SOURCE

In Isaiah 58:2, the Lord said "they ask of me the ordinances (Hebrew *mishpawt*, meaning to judge a verdict) of justice (Hebrew *tsaw-dak*, meaning the right from *tsad-deek*, meaning to be [causal] or to cause right)." The spirit of Justice (Isaiah 4:4, 28:6, 29:24) "sees" what is right. When an act or "responsibility to keep" is lessened, the spirit of Justice "sees" and the human being responds, knowing injustice.

PATHWAY

The spirit of Justice responds to what is seen. Human anger is the physiological response to injustice as seen by the spirit of Justice and Judgment. In the Old Testament, God was angered (Exodus 4:14; Numbers 11:10, 12:9, 22:22, 25:3-4; Deuteronomy 6:15, 29:20, 29:27; Judges 2:14, 3:8, 10:7; 2 Samuel 24:1; 2 Kings 17:11; 24:20; Isaiah 1:4; Jeremiah 4:8, 26, 12:13, 25:37; Zephaniah 2:2). The Old Testament prophets recorded God's anger (Hebrew *aph*, meaning the nose or nostril from *amaph*, meaning to breathe hard, i.e. be enraged) was hot (Hebrew *charah*, meaning to glow). What God saw (injustice) caused His spirit to glow or kindled (Exodus 4:14; Numbers 11:10, 12:9, 22:22, 32:10; Deuteronomy 6:15, 7:4, 11:17, 29:27; Joshua 7:1, 23:16; 2 Samuel 6:7, 24:1; 2 Kings 13:3; 1 Chronicles 13:10; 2 Chronicles 25:15; Psalm 106:40; Isaiah 5:25). [See chapter seven for more insight.]

BEHAVIOR

The essence of the spirit of Justice and Judgment has lit (Genesis 30:2; Numbers 11:1, 22:27, 24:10; Judges 9:30, 14:19; 1 Samuel 11:6, 17:28, 20:30; 2 Samuel 12:5; Job 32:2-5) properties within. The words in the Old Testament which describe anger are not physiological or behavioral but affective spirit descriptors. The spirit may cause anger to burn slow (Nehemiah 9:17; Psalm 103:8, 145:8; Proverbs 14:29, 15:18, 16:23; Joel 2:13; Jonah 4:2; Nahum 1:3), be stirred (Hebrew *alah,* meaning to ascend) (Proverbs 15:1), be burned (Hebrew *ba'ar,* meaning to kindle, i.e. consume) (Esther 1:12), or be waxed hot (Hebrew *halak,* meaning to walk with *charah,* meaning to glow) (Exodus 32:19). The closer Moses came to the camp and saw the calf and dancing, his anger became hot.

The brightness of the glow is determined by the spirit in response to the injustice "seen". The glow may be: great (Hebrew *choriy,* meaning a burning [i.e. intense] anger (Exodus 11:8); provoked (Hebrew *na'ats,* meaning to scorn [i.e. to bloom in expression] (Deuteronomy 4:25, 9:18, 31:29; 1 Kings 14:9, 16:26, 33; 2 Kings 17:11, 17, 21:6, 22:17, 23:19; 2 Chronicles 34:25; Job 12:6; Jeremiah 7:18, 25:7, 32:29, 32; Ezekiel 8:17, 16:26); fierceness or wrathful (Hebrew *charown,* meaning a burning anger [displeasure] (Deuteronomy 13:17; Joshua 7:26; Psalm 78:49, 85:3; Hosea 11:9; Nahum 1:6); fury (Hebrew *chemah,* meaning heat from *yacham, meaning* to be hot) (Isaiah 42:25) or tear perpetually (Hebrew *taraph,* meaning to pluck off [Amos 1:11] and Hebrew *ad,* meaning duration in the sense of advance).

The spirit may also withdraw (Hebrew *shuwb,* meaning to turn back) (Job 9:13), or turn away (Hebrew *shuwb* and *cuwr,* meaning to turn back and turn off), its anger. The spirit may also rest (Hebrew *nuwach,* meaning to rest or settle down) (Ecclesiastes 7:9) or make pacifieth (Hebrew *kaphah,* meaning to bend) (Proverbs 21:14).

Trew and Alden (2009) said there are variations in anger. Such as anger-out which refers to how often an individual expresses angry feelings through verbally or physically aggressive behavior and is associated with pathological outcomes relative to anger-in. Anger-in refers to how often an individual experiences, but holds in (i.e. suppresses), angry feelings and is associated with a variety of internalizing symptoms (e.g. anxiety, depression, interpersonal sensitivity). Burns, Quartana, and Bruehl (2008) suggested the inhibition of anger (anger-in) is believed to be the suppressing or inhibition of the verbal or physical expression of anger and is related to increased pain severity.

R & M Seminars (Ta-tutor.com) describes seven different types of anger. The first is Rebellious anger. This type of anger is a natural developmental process as children define themselves be getting others to resond to them when they are oppositional: Parent says "do," child says, "no,"; parent says, "don't," child does it anyway. The second type is Rachet anger. This type is unhealthy. It is described as chronic and serves as a coverup for vulnerability. Beneath this type of anger are disowned fear, incomplete developmental needs, grief, and potency. The third type is called Pig Parent anger. It is punitive and destructive, homicidal, and suicidal. It is developed in the child by the child protecting himself from adverse external abuse from outside Pig Parents.

The fourth type is called Parent anger. It has health limit setting and Righteous Parent anger believes the parent is doing it for the good of others or the relationship. This type just wants to lash out. The fifth type is Responsive anger. This type helps in setting boundaries and making contact when others are intruding or alienating themselves. The sixth type is adapted anger. It is a natural anger that is interrupted by thinking or fear before it is expressed. The last type is Natural anger. It is biological or natural. When a child feels invaded or abandoned, whether as an infant, older child or an adult.

From the Old Testament, several words are used to express the ventilation of anger. Although different English words are used to express how this emotion is experienced, the means of expression is generally the same.

Kindled = Nose, breathe hard (Exodus 4:14)
Waxed = Nose, breathe hard (Exodus 32:22)
Fierce = Nose, breathe hard (Num. 25:4)
Provoke = To trouble (Deut. 4:25)
Great = Nose, breathe hard (Deut. 29:24)
Hot = Nose, breathe hard (Judges 2:14)
Burned = Heat, to be hot (Es. 1:12)
Withdraw = Nose, breathe hard (Job 9:13)
Endureth = Nose, breathe hard (Ps. 30:5)
Wrathful = Nose, breathe hard (Ps. 69:24)
Smoke = Nose, breathe hard (Ps. 74:1)
Slow = Nose, breathe hard (Ps. 103:3)
Stir up = Nose, breathe hard (Prov. 15:1)
Pacifieth = Nose, breathe hard (Prov. 21:14)
Turned away = Nose, breathe hard (Is. 12:1)
Indignation = Nose, breathe hard (Is. 30:30)
Fury = Nose, breathe hard (Is. 42:25)
Perpetually = Nose, breathe hard (Amos 1:11)
Away = Nose, breathe hard (Prov. 27:9)
Resteth = Vexation [displeasure], to trouble (Ec. 7:9)
Tear = Nose, breathe hard (Amos 1:11)

CONCLUSION

Human anger can be described with many expressions of discomfort. However, the spirit of Justice and Judgment "see" what is right and human behavior is quickly responsive. The essence of the spirit determines the degree of anger in behavior. The spirit provokes or moves the human being to display varying degrees of anger. Just as the spirit "sees" injustice, it also determines the valanced level of anger and the quickness of withdraw. I recommend further research in this area should include a thorough review of data regarding this spirit.

KEY WORDS

1. Human anger
2. Spirit of justice and judgment
3. Turn away anger

KEY QUESTIONS

1. Where does anger come from in the human being?
2. Explain how anger levels are regulated in human beings?

Quick Scripture Reference Guide

Genesis 30:2 (NKJV)

2 And Jacob's anger was aroused against Rachel, and he said, "*Am* I in the place of God, who has withheld from you the fruit of the womb?"

Exodus 4:14 (NKJV)

14 So the anger of the LORD was kindled against Moses, and He said: "Is not Aaron the Levite your brother? I know that he can speak well. And look, he is also coming out to meet you. When he sees you, he will be glad in his heart.

Exodus 11:8 (NKJV)

8 And all these your servants shall come down to me and bow down to me, saying, 'Get out, and all the people who follow you!' After that I will go out." Then he went out from Pharaoh in great anger.

Exodus 32:19 (NKJV)

19 So it was, as soon as he came near the camp, that he saw the calf *and* the dancing. So Moses' anger became hot, and he cast the tablets out of his hands and broke them at the foot of the mountain.

Numbers 11:1 (NKJV)

1 Now *when* the people complained, it displeased the LORD; for the LORD heard *it,* and His anger was aroused. So the fire of the LORD burned among them, and consumed *some* in the outskirts of the camp.

Numbers 11:10 (NKJV)

10 Then Moses heard the people weeping throughout their families, everyone at the door of his tent; and the anger of the LORD was greatly aroused; Moses also was displeased.

Numbers 12:9-10 (NKJV)

9 So the anger of the LORD was aroused against them, and He departed.

10 And when the cloud departed from above the tabernacle, suddenly Miriam *became* leprous, as *white as* snow. Then Aaron turned toward Miriam, and there she was, a leper.

Numbers 22:22 (NKJV)

22 Then God's anger was aroused because he went, and the Angel of the LORD took His stand in the way as an adversary against him. And he was riding on his donkey, and his two servants *were* with him.

Numbers 22:27 (NKJV)

27 And when the donkey saw the Angel of the LORD, she lay down under Balaam; so Balaam's anger was aroused, and he struck the donkey with his staff.

Numbers 24:10 (NKJV)

10 Then Balak's anger was aroused against Balaam, and he struck his hands together; and Balak said to Balaam, "I called you to curse my enemies, and look, you have bountifully blessed *them* these three times!

Numbers 25:2-4 (NKJV)

2 They invited the people to the sacrifices of their gods, and the people ate and bowed down to their gods.

3 So Israel was joined to Baal of Peor, and the anger of the LORD was aroused against Israel.

4 Then the LORD said to Moses, "Take all the leaders of the people and hang the offenders before the LORD, out in the sun, that the fierce anger of the LORD may turn away from Israel."

Numbers 32:10 (NKJV)

10 So the LORD'S anger was aroused on that day, and He swore an oath, saying,

Deuteronomy 4:25 (NKJV)

25 "When you beget children and grandchildren and have grown old in the land, and act corruptly and make a carved image in the form of anything, and do evil in the sight of the LORD your God to provoke Him to anger,

Deuteronomy 6:15 (NKJV)

15 (for the LORD your God *is* a jealous God among you), lest the anger of the LORD your God be aroused against you and destroy you from the face of the earth.

Deuteronomy 7:4 (NKJV)

4 For they will turn your sons away from following Me, to serve other gods; so the anger of the LORD will be aroused against you and destroy you suddenly.

Deuteronomy 9:18 (NKJV)

18 And I fell down before the LORD, as at the first, forty days and forty nights; I neither ate bread nor drank water, because of all your sin which you committed in doing wickedly in the sight of the LORD, to provoke Him to anger.

Deuteronomy 11:17 (NKJV)

17 lest the LORD'S anger be aroused against you, and He shut up the heavens so that there be no rain, and the land yield no produce, and you perish quickly from the good land which the LORD is giving you.

Deuteronomy 13:17 (NKJV)

17 So none of the accursed things shall remain in your hand, that the LORD may turn from the fierceness of His anger and show you mercy, have compassion on you and multiply you, just as He swore to your fathers,

Deuteronomy 29:20 (NKJV)

20 The LORD would not spare him; for then the anger of the LORD and His jealousy would burn against that man, and every curse that is written in this book would settle on him, and the LORD would blot out his name from under heaven.

Deuteronomy 29:27 (NKJV)

[27] Then the anger of the LORD was aroused against this land, to bring on it every curse that is written in this book.

Deuteronomy 31:29 (NKJV)

[29] For I know that after my death you will become utterly corrupt, and turn aside from the way which I have commanded you; and evil will befall you in the latter days, because you will do evil in the sight of the LORD, to provoke Him to anger through the work of your hands."

Joshua 7:1 (NKJV)

[1] But the children of Israel committed a trespass regarding the accursed things, for Achan the son of Carmi, the son of Zabdi, the son of Zerah, of the tribe of Judah, took of the accursed things; so the anger of the LORD burned against the children of Israel.

Joshua 7:26 (NKJV)

[26] Then they raised over him a great heap of stones, still there to this day. So the LORD turned from the fierceness of His anger. Therefore the name of that place has been called the Valley of Achor to this day.

Joshua 23:16 (NKJV)

[16] When you have transgressed the covenant of the LORD your God, which He commanded you, and have gone and served other gods, and bowed down to them, then the anger of the LORD will burn against you, and you shall perish quickly from the good land which He has given you."

Judges 2:14 (NKJV)

[14] And the anger of the LORD was hot against Israel. So He delivered them into the hands of plunderers who despoiled them; and He sold them into the hands of their enemies all around, so that they could no longer stand before their enemies.

Judges 3:8 (NKJV)

[8] Therefore the anger of the LORD was hot against Israel, and He sold them into the hand of Cushan-Rishathaim king of Mesopotamia; and the children of Israel served Cushan-Rishathaim eight years.

Judges 9:3 (NKJV)

[3] And his mother's brothers spoke all these words concerning him in the hearing of all the men of Shechem; and their heart was inclined to follow Abimelech, for they said, "He is our brother."

Judges 10:7 (NKJV)

[7] So the anger of the LORD was hot against Israel; and He sold them into the hands of the Philistines and into the hands of the people of Ammon.

Judges 14:19 (NKJV)

[19] Then the Spirit of the LORD came upon him mightily, and he went down to Ashkelon and killed thirty of their men, took their apparel, and gave the changes *of clothing* to those who had explained the riddle. So his anger was aroused, and he went back up to his father's house.

1 Samuel 11:6 (NKJV)

[6] Then the Spirit of God came upon Saul when he heard this news, and his anger was greatly aroused.

1 Samuel 17:28 (NKJV)

[28] Now Eliab his oldest brother heard when he spoke to the men; and Eliab's anger was aroused against David, and he said, "Why did you come down here? And with whom have you left those few sheep in the wilderness? I know your pride and the insolence of your heart, for you have come down to see the battle."

1 Samuel 20:30 (NKJV)

30 Then Saul's anger was aroused against Jonathan, and he said to him, "You son of a perverse, rebellious *woman!* Do I not know that you have chosen the son of Jesse to your own shame and to the shame of your mother's nakedness?

2 Samuel 6:7 (NKJV)

7 Then the anger of the LORD was aroused against Uzzah, and God struck him there for *his* error; and he died there by the ark of God.

2 Samuel 12:5 (NKJV)

5 So David's anger was greatly aroused against the man, and he said to Nathan, "*As* the LORD lives, the man who has done this shall surely die!

2 Samuel 24:1 (NKJV)

1 Again the anger of the LORD was aroused against Israel, and He moved David against them to say, "Go, number Israel and Judah."

1 Kings 14:9 (NKJV)

9 but you have done more evil than all who were before you, for you have gone and made for yourself other gods and molded images to provoke Me to anger, and have cast Me behind your back–

1 Kings 16:26 (NKJV)

26 For he walked in all the ways of Jeroboam the son of Nebat, and in his sin by which he had made Israel sin, provoking the LORD God of Israel to anger with their idols.

1 Kings 16:33 (NKJV)

33 And Ahab made a wooden image. Ahab did more to provoke the LORD God of Israel to anger than all the kings of Israel who were before him.

2 Kings 13:3 (NKJV)

3 Then the anger of the LORD was aroused against Israel, and He delivered them into the hand of Hazael king of Syria, and into the hand of Ben-Hadad the son of Hazael, all *their* days.

2 Kings 17:11 (NKJV)

11 There they burned incense on all the high places, like the nations whom the LORD had carried away before them; and they did wicked things to provoke the LORD to anger,

2 Kings 17:17 (NKJV)

17 And they caused their sons and daughters to pass through the fire, practiced witchcraft and soothsaying, and sold themselves to do evil in the sight of the LORD, to provoke Him to anger.

2 Kings 21:6 (NKJV)

6 Also he made his son pass through the fire, practiced soothsaying, used witchcraft, and consulted spiritists and mediums. He did much evil in the sight of the LORD, to provoke *Him* to anger.

2 Kings 22:17 (NKJV)

17 because they have forsaken Me and burned incense to other gods, that they might provoke Me to anger with all the works of their hands. Therefore My wrath shall be aroused against this place and shall not be quenched.' " '

2 Kings 23:19 (NKJV)

19 Now Josiah also took away all the shrines of the high places that *were* in the cities of Samaria, which the kings of Israel had made to provoke the LORD to anger; and he did to them according to all the deeds he had done in Bethel.

2 Kings 24:20 (NKJV)

[20] For because of the anger of the LORD *this* happened in Jerusalem and Judah, that He finally cast them out from His presence. Then Zedekiah rebelled against the king of Babylon.

1 Chronicles 13:10 (NKJV)

[10] Then the anger of the LORD was aroused against Uzza, and He struck him because he put his hand to the ark; and he died there before God.

2 Chronicles 25:15 (NKJV)

[15] Therefore the anger of the LORD was aroused against Amaziah, and He sent him a prophet who said to him, "Why have you sought the gods of the people, which could not rescue their own people from your hand?"

2 Chronicles 34:25 (NKJV)

[25] because they have forsaken Me and burned incense to other gods, that they might provoke Me to anger with all the works of their hands. Therefore My wrath will be poured out on this place, and not be quenched.' " '

Nehemiah 9:17 (NKJV)

[17] They refused to obey, And they were not mindful of Your wonders That You did among them. But they hardened their necks, And in their rebellion They appointed a leader To return to their bondage. But You *are* God, Ready to pardon, Gracious and merciful, Slow to anger, Abundant in kindness, And did not forsake them.

Esther 1:12 (NKJV)

[12] But Queen Vashti refused to come at the king's command *brought* by *his* eunuchs; therefore the king was furious, and his anger burned within him.

Job 9:13 (NKJV)

[13] God will not withdraw His anger, The allies of the proud lie prostrate beneath Him.

Job 12:6 (NKJV)

6 The tents of robbers prosper, And those who provoke God are secure– In what God provides by His hand.

Job 32:2-5 (NKJV)

2 Then the wrath of Elihu, the son of Barachel the Buzite, of the family of Ram, was aroused against Job; his wrath was aroused because he justified himself rather than God.

3 Also against his three friends his wrath was aroused, because they had found no answer, and *yet* had condemned Job.

4 Now because they *were* years older than he, Elihu had waited to speak to Job.

5 When Elihu saw that *there was* no answer in the mouth of these three men, his wrath was aroused.

Psalm 78:49 (NKJV)

49 He cast on them the fierceness of His anger, Wrath, indignation, and trouble, By sending angels of destruction *among them.*

Psalm 85:3 (NKJV)

3 You have taken away all Your wrath; You have turned from the fierceness of Your anger.

Psalm 103:8 (NKJV)

8 The LORD *is* merciful and gracious, Slow to anger, and abounding in mercy.

Psalm 106:40 (NKJV)

40 Therefore the wrath of the LORD was kindled against His people, So that He abhorred His own inheritance.

Psalm 145:8 (NKJV)

[8] The LORD *is* gracious and full of compassion, Slow to anger and great in mercy.

Proverbs 14:29 (NKJV)

[29] *He who is* slow to wrath has great understanding, But *he who is* impulsive exalts folly.

Proverbs 15:1 (NKJV)

[1] A soft answer turns away wrath, But a harsh word stirs up anger.

Proverbs 15:18 (NKJV)

[18] A wrathful man stirs up strife, But *he who is* slow to anger allays contention.

Proverbs 16:23 (NKJV)

[23] The heart of the wise teaches his mouth, And adds learning to his lips.

Proverbs 21:14 (NKJV)

[14] A gift in secret pacifies anger, And a bribe behind the back, strong wrath.

Ecclesiastes 7:9 (NKJV)

[9] Do not hasten in your spirit to be angry, For anger rests in the bosom of fools.

Isaiah 1:4 (NKJV)

[4] Alas, sinful nation, A people laden with iniquity, A brood of evildoers, Children who are corrupters! They have forsaken the LORD, They have provoked to anger The Holy One of Israel, They have turned away backward.

Isaiah 4:4 (NKJV)

[4] When the Lord has washed away the filth of the daughters of Zion, and purged the blood of Jerusalem from her midst, by the spirit of judgment and by the spirit of burning,

Isaiah 5:25 (NKJV)

[25] Therefore the anger of the LORD is aroused against His people; He has stretched out His hand against them And stricken them, And the hills trembled. Their carcasses *were* as refuse in the midst of the streets. For all this His anger is not turned away, But His hand *is* stretched out still.

Isaiah 28:6 (NKJV)

[6] For a spirit of justice to him who sits in judgment, And for strength to those who turn back the battle at the gate.

Isaiah 29:24 (NKJV)

[24] These also who erred in spirit will come to understanding, And those who complained will learn doctrine."

Isaiah 42:25 (NKJV)

[25] Therefore He has poured on him the fury of His anger And the strength of battle; It has set him on fire all around, Yet he did not know; And it burned him, Yet he did not take *it* to heart.

Isaiah 58:2 (NKJV)

[2] Yet they seek Me daily, And delight to know My ways, As a nation that did righteousness, And did not forsake the ordinance of their God. They ask of Me the ordinances of justice; They take delight in approaching God.

Jeremiah 4:8 (NKJV)

[8] For this, clothe yourself with sackcloth, Lament and wail. For the fierce anger of the LORD Has not turned back from us.

Jeremiah 4:26 (NKJV)

[26] I beheld, and indeed the fruitful land *was* a wilderness, And all its cities were broken down At the presence of the LORD, By His fierce anger.

Jeremiah 12:13 (NKJV)

13 They have sown wheat but reaped thorns; They have put themselves to pain *but* do not profit. But be ashamed of your harvest Because of the fierce anger of the LORD."

Jeremiah 7:18 (NKJV)

18 The children gather wood, the fathers kindle the fire, and the women knead dough, to make cakes for the queen of heaven; and *they* pour out drink offerings to other gods, that they may provoke Me to anger.

Jeremiah 25:7 (NKJV)

7 Yet you have not listened to Me," says the LORD, "that you might provoke Me to anger with the works of your hands to your own hurt.

Jeremiah 25:37 (NKJV)

37 And the peaceful dwellings are cut down Because of the fierce anger of the LORD.

Jeremiah 32:29 (NKJV)

29 And the Chaldeans who fight against this city shall come and set fire to this city and burn it, with the houses on whose roofs they have offered incense to Baal and poured out drink offerings to other gods, to provoke Me to anger;

Jeremiah 32:32 (NKJV)

32 because of all the evil of the children of Israel and the children of Judah, which they have done to provoke Me to anger–they, their kings, their princes, their priests, their prophets, the men of Judah, and the inhabitants of Jerusalem.

Ezekiel 8:17 (NKJV)

17 And He said to me, "Have you seen *this,* O son of man? Is it a trivial thing to the house of Judah to commit the abominations which they commit here? For they have filled the land with violence; then they have returned to provoke Me to anger. Indeed they put the branch to their nose.

Ezekiel 16:26 (NKJV)

26 You also committed harlotry with the Egyptians, your very fleshly neighbors, and increased your acts of harlotry to provoke Me to anger.

Hosea 11:9 (NKJV)

9 I will not execute the fierceness of My anger; I will not again destroy Ephraim. For I *am* God, and not man, The Holy One in your midst; And I will not come with terror.

Joel 2:13 (NKJV)

13 So rend your heart, and not your garments; Return to the LORD your God, For He *is* gracious and merciful, Slow to anger, and of great kindness; And He relents from doing harm.

Amos 1:11 (NKJV)

11 Thus says the LORD: "For three transgressions of Edom, and for four, I will not turn away its *punishment,* Because he pursued his brother with the sword, And cast off all pity; His anger tore perpetually, And he kept his wrath forever.

Jonah 4:2 (NKJV)

2 So he prayed to the LORD, and said, "Ah, LORD, was not this what I said when I was still in my country? Therefore I fled previously to Tarshish; for I know that You *are* a gracious and merciful God, slow to anger and abundant in lovingkindness, One who relents from doing harm.

Nahum 1:3 (NKJV)

3 The LORD *is* slow to anger and great in power, And will not at all acquit *the wicked.* The LORD has His way In the whirlwind and in the storm, And the clouds *are* the dust of His feet.

Nahum 1:6 (NKJV)

6 Who can stand before His indignation? And who can endure the fierceness of His anger? His fury is poured out like fire, And the rocks are thrown down by Him.

Zephaniah 2:2 (NKJV)

[2] Before the decree is issued, *Or* the day passes like chaff, Before the LORD'S fierce anger comes upon you, Before the day of the LORD'S anger comes upon you!

Chapter Fifteen – The Pathway of Happy

SOURCE

This is a very short chapter because there is limited information on this emotion in the scriptures. Malachi (3:13-15) described the behavior of people as useless to serve God; "What profit is it that we have kept His ordinance and that we have walked as mourners before the Lord of hosts?" The proud are called happy (Hebrew *ashar,* meaning to be straight). To be straight, there must be two causal factors in place. The spirit must see from two factors which cause happy. First, the spirit "sees" slow (Hebrew *kabed,* meaning heavy as numerous, from Hebrew *kabad,* meaning causal, to make weighty). Second, the spirit "sees" laughter (Hebrew *sechowq,* meaning laughter, from Hebrew *sachaq,* meaning to laugh).

PATHWAY

In Genesis 21:6, Sarah said "God has made (Hebrew *asah,* meaning to do or make) me laugh" (Hebrew *tsechoq,* meaning laughter [in pleasure] from Hebrew *tsachaq,* meaning to laugh outright). Sarah added, "all that hear (Hebrew *shama,* meaning to hear intelligently) will laugh with me". The cognitive affect of hearing laughter prompts automatization, i.e. the repetition of a sequence of thoughts and actions until it becomes automatic (Berger, 2008). If Berger is right, then hearing other people laugh prompts others to laugh. If you accept the scriptures are absolute, then, the spirit in each human being prompts laughter.

BEHAVIOR

The scriptures state you will be happy when you work with your hands (Psalm 128:2), when an injustice to others is repaid (Psalm 137:8-9), when individuals and people make God their Lord (Psalm 144:15), when the people of God hope in God (Psalm 146:5), when you find wisdom and understanding (Proverbs 3:13), when you retain your newly gained wisdom and understanding (Proverbs 3:18), when you give mercy to the needy (Proverbs 14:21), when you trust in the Lord (Proverbs 16:20), when you dread the consequences of sin (Proverbs 28:14), and when you keep God's word (Proverbs 28:18).

Happiness is not dependent upon chronological age or adult maturation. The spirit in each person "sees" and behaves happily. This emotion is determined by the spirit seeing and human behavior manifests happy when slow laughter is seen. Laughter may be in pleasure or detraction, i.e. a lessening of esteem (Merriam-Webster, 2003).

CONCLUSION

Happy is an emotion caused by a spirit. Scriptures do not state which spirit causes this emotion, but that it is of the spirit.

KEY WORDS

1. Happy

KEY QUESTIONS

1. What must the spirit "see" to cause a human being to be happy?
2. How is this emotion in human beings determined by a spirit?

Quick Scripture Reference Guide

Genesis 21:6 (NKJV)

6 And Sarah said, "God has made me laugh, *and* all who hear will laugh with me."

Psalm 128:2 (NKJV)

2 When you eat the labor of your hands, You *shall be* happy, and *it shall be* well with you.

Psalm 137:8-9 (NKJV)

8 O daughter of Babylon, who are to be destroyed, Happy the one who repays you as you have served us!

9 Happy the one who takes and dashes Your little ones against the rock!

Psalm 144:15 (NKJV)

15 Happy *are* the people who are in such a state; Happy *are* the people whose God *is* the LORD!

Psalm 146:5 (NKJV)

5 Happy *is he* who *has* the God of Jacob for his help, Whose hope *is* in the LORD his God,

Proverbs 3:13 (NKJV)

13 Happy *is* the man *who* finds wisdom, And the man *who* gains understanding;

Proverbs 3:18 (NKJV)

18 She *is* a tree of life to those who take hold of her, And happy *are all* who retain her.

Proverbs 14:21 (NKJV)

[21] He who despises his neighbor sins; But he who has mercy on the poor, happy *is* he.

Proverbs 16:20 (NKJV)

[20] He who heeds the word wisely will find good, And whoever trusts in the LORD, happy *is* he.

Proverbs 28:14 (NKJV)

[14] Happy *is* the man who is always reverent, But he who hardens his heart will fall into calamity.

Proverbs 28:18 (NKJV)

[18] Whoever walks blamelessly will be saved, But *he who is* perverse *in his* ways will suddenly fall.

Malachi 3:13-15 (NKJV)

[13] "Your words have been harsh against Me," Says the LORD, "Yet you say, 'What have we spoken against You?'

[14] You have said, 'It is useless to serve God; What profit *is it* that we have kept His ordinance, And that we have walked as mourners Before the LORD of hosts?

[15] So now we call the proud blessed, For those who do wickedness are raised up; They even tempt God and go free.' "

References

Ahlstrom, Gerd (2007). Experiences of loss and chronic sorrow in persons with severe chronic illness, *Journal of Nursing and Healthcare of Chronic Illness, Journal of Clinical Nursing*, 16(3a)

Beer, Jennifer, S., Lombardo, Michael, V. (2008). Insights into Emotion Regulations from Neuropsychology, Emotion Regulation, The Handbook of Emotions, Lewis, Haviland-Jones, Barrett, Guilford Press, New York

Berger, Kathleen, Stassen (2008). The Developing Person, through the life Span, Worth Publishers, New York, New York, pp 4

Berghash, Rachel, Jillson, Katherine (1998). Thoughts on Psyche, Soul, and Spirit, *Journal of Religion and Health,* 37(4)

Burns, John W., Quartana, Phillip, J., Bruehl, Stephen (2008). Anger inhibition and pain: conceptualizations, evidence and new directions, *Journal of Behavioral Medicine,* 31

Carter, John, D. and Narramore, Bruce (1979). The Integration of Psychology and Theology, The Rosemead Psychology Series, Zondervan, Grand Rapids, Michigan

Chapple, Constance, L., Johnson, Katherine, A. (2007). Gender Differences in Impulsivity, *Journal of Youth Violence and Juvenile Justice*, 5(3)

Craig, Grace, J., Baucum, Don (2002). Human Development, (9th ed.) Upper Saddle River, New Jersey, Prentice Hall, 115-155, 228

DeSteno, David; Valdesolo, Piercarlo; & Bartlett, Monica, Y. (2006). *Journal of Personality and social Psychology*, 91(4)

DSM-IV-TR (4th ed.)(2000). Diagnostic and Statistical Manuela of Mental Disorders, American Psychiatric Association, Washington, DC

Eakes, Georgene, G., Burke, Mary, L. (1999). Chronic Sorrow: The experiences of Bereaved Individuals, Crises & Loss, 7(2).

*Fischer, Agneta, H., Manstead, Antony, S.R. (*2008). Social Funcitons of Emotion, The Handbook of Emotions, Lewis, Haviland-Jones, Barrett, Guilford Press, New York

Frijda, Nico, H. (2008). The Psychophysiology of Emotion, The Handbook of Emotions, Lewis, Haviland-Jones, Barrett, Guilford Press, New York

Fridja, Nico,H. (2008). The Psychologists' Point of View, The Handbook of Emotions, Lewis, Haviland-Jones, Barrett, Guilford Press, New York

Gilliland, Burl, E., James, Richard, K. (1998). Theories and Strategies in Counseling and Psychotherapy,(4th ed.), A Viacom company, Needham Heights, Ma, pp 237

Gross, James, J. (2008). Emotion Regulation, The Handbook of Emotions, Lewis, Haviland-Jones, Barrett, Guilford Press, New York

Guerrero, Laura, K. Trost, Melanie, R. and Yoshimura, Stephen, M. (2005). Romantic jealousy: Emotions and communicative responses, *Journal of Personal Relationships*, 12

Hall, Calvin, S., Lindzey, Gardner (1957). Theories of Personality, John Wiley and Sons, Inc, New York, pp 482

Harrison, R.K. (Ed.), Vos, Howard, K & Barber, Cyril, J. (Contributing Ed.), Unger, Merrill, F. (1988). The New Unger's Bible Dictionary, Moody Press, Chicago, Illinois

Helminiak, Daniel (1996). A Scientific Spirituality: The interface of Psychology and Theology, *The International Journal for the Psychology of Religion,* 6(1)

Helminiak, Daniel, A. (1998). Sexuality and Spirituality: A Humanist Account. *Pastoral Psychology*, 47(2)

Johnson-Laird, P.N. and Oatley, Keith (2008). Emotions, Music, and Literature, The Handbook of Emotions, Lewis, Haviland-Jones, Barrett, Guilford Press, New York

Jones, Stanton, L., Butman, Richard, E. (1991). A Comprehensive Christian appraisal, Modern Psycho-Therapies, Intervarsity Press, Downers Grove, Illinois

Kottler, Jeffery, A., Brown, Robert, W. (2000). Introduction to Therapeutic Counseling, voices from the field, Brooks/Cole, Thomson Learning, (4th ed.), Belmont, CA, pp 145

Larsen, Jeff, T., Berntson, Gary, G., Poehlmann, Kirsten, M., Ito, Tiffany, A., and Cacioppo, John, T. (2008). The Psychophysiology of Emotion, The Handbook of Emotions, Lewis, Haviland-Jones, Barrett, Guilford Press, New York

Ledoux, Joseph; Phelps, Elizabeth, A. (2008). Emotional Networks in the Brain, The Handbook of Emotions, Lewis, Haviland-Jones, Barrett, Guilford Press, New York

Lewis, Michael (2008). The Emergence of Human Emotions, The Handbook of Emotions, Lewis, Haviland-Jones, Barrett, Guilford Press, New York

Libet, B. (1994). Neurophysiology of consciousness: Selected papers and new essays. Birkhauswer

Lindren, C.L., Burke, M.L., Hainsworth, M.A., and Eakes, G.G. (1992). Chronic Sorrow: A lifespan concept, Scholarly Inquiry for Nursing Practice, 6(27-40).

MacArthur, John (2003). Think Biblically, Recovering a Christian Worldview, Wheaton, Illinois, Crossway books, 55

Maxmen, Jerrold, S. Ward, Nicholas, G. (1995). Essential Psychopathology and its treatment, Norton, New York

Mele, Alfed, R. (1997). Real self-deception, *Journal of Behavioral and Brain Sciences*, 20, 91-136

Merriam-Webster Collegiate Dictionary (11th ed.) (2007). Springfield, MA: Merriam-Webster

Palmer, Parker, J. (2003). Teaching with heart and soul, reflections on spirituality in teacher education, *Journal of Teacher Education*, 54(5)

Panksepp, Jaak (2008). The Affective Brain and Core Consciousness, The Handbook of Emotions, Lewis, Haviland-Jones, Barrett, Guilford Press, New York

Pfeiffer, Susan, M. and Wong, Paul, T.P. (1989). Multidimensional jealousy, *Journal of Social and Personal Relationships*, 6

Pink, Arthur(1930). The Sovereignty of God, Bible Truth Depot, Swengel, Pa.

Puente, Sylvia; Cohen, Dov (2003). Jealousy and the meaning (or nonmeaning) of violence, *Society for Personality and Social Psychology*, 29(4)

Quirk, Gregory, J. (2008). Prefrontal-Amygdala Interactions in the Regulation of Fear, Emotion Regulation, The Handbook of Emotions, Lewis, Haviland-Jones, Barrett, Guilford Press, New York

R & M Seminars (1995). Anger – 7 Kinds, Relationship & mangagement, Lewis Quinby, Eureka, Ca., http://www.ta-tutor.com.html

Sagarin, Grad, J., Guadagnpo, Rosanna, E. (2004). Sex differences in the contexts of extreme jealousy, *Journal of Personal Relationships*, 11

Sharf, Richard, S. (2000). Theories of Psychotherapy & Counseling, Concepts and Cases, (2nd ed.), Brooks/Cole, Thomson Learning, Belmont, CA, pp 507

Siegman, Aron, Wolfe and Snow, Selena, Cappell (1997). The Outward expression of anger, the inward experience of anger and CVR: The role of vocal expression, 20(1)

Smith, Eliot, Mackie, Diane, M. (2008). Intergroup Emotions, The Handbook of Emotions, Lewis, Haviland-Jones, Barrett, Guilford Press, New York

Solomon, Robert, C. (2008). The Philosophy of Emotions, The Handbook of Emotions, Lewis, Haviland-Jones, Barrett, Guilford Press, New York

Sperry, Len (1995). Handbook of Diagnosis and Treatment of the DSM-IV Personality Disorders, Brunner/Mazel, Levittown, PA

Stearns, Peter, N. (2008). History of Emotions, The Handbook of Emotions, Lewis, Haviland-Jones, Barrett, Guilford Press, New York

Stets, jan, E., Turner, Jonathan, H. (2008). The Sociology of Emotions, The Handbook of Emotions, Lewis, Haviland-Jones, Barrett, Guilford Press, New York

Strong, James. Strong's Exhaustive Concordance of the Bible, with brief Dictionaries of the Hebrew and Greek words of the original with references to the English words.

Thiessen, Henry, C. (1989). Lectures in Systematic Theology, William Eerdmans Publishing, pp. 163

Tooby, John, Cosmides, Leda (2008). The Evolutionary Psychology of Emotions and their Relationship to Internal Regulatory Variables, The Handbook of Emotions, Lewis, Haviland-Jones, Barrett, Guilford Press, New York

Towns, Elmer (2001). Theology for today, Thomson Publishing, 10-11, 588

Trew, Jennifer, Alden, Lynn, E. (2009). Predicting anger in social anxiety: the mediating role of rumination, Behavior Research and Therapy, 47

Wager, Tor, D., Barrett, Lisa, Feldman, Bliss-Moreau, Elisa, Lindquist, Kristen, A., Duncan, Seth, Kober, Hedy,Joseph, Josh, Davidson, Mattthew, and Mize, Jennifer (2008). The Neuroimaging of Emotion, The Handbook of Emotions, Lewis, Haviland-Jones, Barrett, Guilford Press, New York

White, Gerry (2007). Dimension: Visions, Dream Interpretation, and Physics, Chapman Printing, West Virginia

Willard, Dallas (1998). The Divine conspiracy, Rediscovering our hidden life in God, Harper, San Francisco

ACKNOWLEDGEMENTS

THE QUALITY OF THIS BOOK is a testament to the skills and abilities of several people and I am very thankful and appreciative for the following individuals who have contributed to the development of this book.

These people are friends of mine and I am grateful to them for spending countless hours in reading this manuscript. They have been gracious with their comments and recommendations.

Manuscript Reviewers

Greg Cook, D.Th.
Andrew Counts, MA., L.P.C.
Bill Ellis, M. DIV, MA, D. D.
Dennis Frey, Th.D.
Shelley Hensley, MD
Gene Mitchell, BS
Donna Paxson, Administrative Secretary
Rodney Taylor, Ed. D.

About the Author

Gerry D. White, D.B.S., is a pastor in West Virginia. He is an assistant professor at Mountwest Community and Technical College in Huntington, West Virginia. He received his Doctorate in Biblical Studies in Biblical Counseling at Master's International School of Divinity. He received his MAR from Liberty Baptist Theological Seminary in Lynchburg, Virginia. He is the author of two books entitled *The Pastor's Collection: Visions* and *Dimension: Visions, Dream Interpretation & Physics.*

In addition to my education, I have included information gained through years of study in the scriptures. I have also included personal knowledge gained by walking with God. Although God has closed the canon of revelation known as the Old Testament and New Testament, God continues to speak through dreams and visions (Job 33: 14-15), pain, i.e. physical sickness (Job 33:19), prayer (Job 33:26), the Holy Spirit (John 16:13), and the Scriptures (2 Timothy 3:16-17).

As you can imagine my educational journey has included two tracts, one in Theology and one in Psychology. Theology is the study of God and Psychology is the study of behavior and mental processes. Recently, books on integration have been written to bridge Theology and Psychology, while some authors suggest it is impossible to build this bridge. There are opposing issues on both sides with each stating their case with very little movement towards integration.

However, some writers are trying to integrate both showing the plausibility and effectual emergence that it has a significant benefit to everyone. While others refuse to build a bridge noting that theology and psychology do not mix. Within this divide man looks within!

www.ingramcontent.com/pod-product-compliance
Lightning Source LLC
LaVergne TN
LVHW070117110826
845147LV00002B/143